Towards European Management

Keith Thurley (LSE)

Hans Wirdenius (FArådet)

Pitman

Pitman Publishing
128 Long Acre, London WC2E 9AN

A Division of Longman Group UK Limited

First published in Great Britain 1989

© Keith Thurley and Hans Wirdenius 1989

British Library Cataloguing in Publication Data

Thurley, Keith
 Towards European management
 I. Title II. Wirdenius, Hans
 658

 ISBN 0-273-03125-2

Printed in Great Britain at The Bath Press, Avon

Towards European Management

Contents

Preface *vii*

Summary of the argument *xi*

1 The meaning of 'European management' 1

1.1   A starting point
1.2   Defining 'European Management'
1.3   The 1992 campaign
1.4   The legacy of cultural pessimism
1.5   The need for organizational change
1.6   The 'Company Doctor' solution
1.7   A general diagnosis

2 The age of the guru: chasing after straws 16

2.1   The American invasions
2.2   Why are there management gurus?
2.3   American management versus Japanese management
2.4   Demand for quick-fix solutions
2.5   Skill at adapting new ideas

3 The study of management practice 25

3.1   What is a manager?
3.2   The failure of empirical research on managerial roles
3.3   A suggested framework: definition of management

4 The gap in management theory 31

4.1   Prescription versus analysis
4.2   Types of management theory
4.3   What is missing?

5 The management of change 41

5.1   The basis for a European approach
5.2   A framework for considering the management of change

**6 Enterprise management: strategic choice in transforming
organizations 48**

6.1   Different forms of enterprise management
6.2   Strategic choice
6.3   Designing a strategy
6.4   Testing the model

7 Taking production seriously 63

7.1   The social context of 'production systems' in Europe
7.2   The functions of supervisory management
7.3   Four approaches to improving supervisory management
7.4   Directions of change: a diagnostic experiment
7.5   An overall approach for regenerating supervisory management

8 The European answer: conditions for success 86

8.1   The long march
8.2   Continuity and innovation
8.3   Choices
8.4   The European management model
8.5   On being a European manager

References 103

Appendix 113

Index 118

Preface

All *serious* books are difficult to write and produce and this volume was very far from an exception. The main ideas behind the book emerged from the experience of twenty-seven years of close collaboration between the authors on a number of projects in applied social research on work organization and behaviour. The framework used comes from these projects. It was not easy to create as the authors come from different disciplines and from cultures which are distinct and different in many subtle ways. The English language is widely used throughout Europe but the meanings attached to words can be very different to those current in the United Kingdom. A 'cross-cultural' book has to be based on the creation of a vocabulary of key concepts with shared meanings which then have to be communicated back to those within the original cultures. A book on 'European management' has to do more than this as it has to make sense to those within more than a dozen cultures. This is clearly a difficult task and we cannot claim to achieve anything more than, hopefully, a promising start.

Realistically, such a start comes mostly from a detailed knowledge of the Scandinavian and British managerial situations and this bias in perspective should be recognized. In recent years, however, the authors have been involved in research projects and teaching in several European countries and in particular grateful acknowledgements should be given for the stimulation and ideas provided by colleagues in the current European Foundation Project on the Changing Roles and Functions of Lower and Middle Management. This must include Jørn Pedersen (European Foundation), Flemming Agersnap (Denmark), Serge Alecian (France), Guiseppe Della Rocca (Italy), Eric Andriessen (Netherlands), Rosemary Stewart (UK), Wolfgang Staehle (West Germany) and Ricardo Peccei (LSE).

The arguments in the book were tested in a special course for business studies undergraduates run by the authors in the Spring

Semester (1988) of the Copenhagen School of Economics. Thanks are due to all the students on the course and the support of Flemming Agersnap and many colleagues from the Institute of Organization and Industrial Sociology at the School. FArådet, stressing the international perspective in research, provides a favourable environment for work and idea exchange across borders, and we are very grateful for having benefited from this when working on the book.

It is also important to thank all friends and research colleagues who have directly contributed to the ideas in this book, especially Pjotr Hesseling (Erasmus University, Rotterdam), Tom Lyons (Irish Productivity Centre, Dublin), Desmond Graves (Templeton College, Oxford), Henri Claude de Bettignies (INSEAD), Finn Strandgaard (Network, Copenhagen), Bob King (ICI) and Rolf Lundin (Umeå University, Umeå). We are particularly grateful for the help received in preparing the book from Annie Robinson (Pitmans) and Pia Jäärf (FArådet).

European management is a term which invites a sceptical response. How can such an animal exist? Clearly, it is not easy to find or define common elements in managerial practice which are unique to work organizations operating in Western Europe.

The approach adopted here is to use the term as a short-hand expression to denote the *search* which is now under way to try to find answers to the following questions:

(*a*) Is it possible to distinguish a specific European approach to management in contrast with American and Japanese competing managerial philosophies?

(*b*) What type of strategies of change are required within the European context in order to achieve a more effective organizational response to world competition?

(*c*) What can be learnt from applied social scientific research on the nature of organizational failures in the European context and their implications for managerial roles?

(*d*) Given the advent of the 1992 Single European Market and the different historical and cultural traditions among European nations, on what basis can the management of European organizations be reformed?

Such questions arise from the specific political, economic and cultural challenges facing European firms, communities and individuals in the transitional years of the 1990s as a new European state is painfully being evolved. It should be made clear that the starting point for our thinking is the possible role for management within this new political context. Management is assumed here to be too important within high technology and advanced societies to be seen as an issue merely of technique or a problem just of organizational efficiency. One of the main barriers to solving such issues is the narrow framework within which business schools throughout the world discuss managerial questions. Leadership, for example, is analysed in terms of social psychological concepts of management style. Corporate strategy decisions are seen as mainly relating to product market requirements. Contingency theory is used to demonstrate the need for a relativist approach in which even organizational culture is seen as reflecting top management decisions on the requirements for organizational survival and growth.

The fact that every organization is different and faces different demands and requirements should not obscure the reality that managerial decisions and choices are not simply about the rational use of resources. There is, of course, a view expressed by several management writers that managerial authority is only legitimate if it is confined to such rational organizational decisions. This is, however, an ideological position related to the view of neoclassists such as Lionel Robbins that economics deals with the use of resources to *given* ends. The reality, in all societies, is that managerial choices reflect social, cultural, political and philosophical beliefs and world-views. In Western and Eastern Europe this is both recognized and accepted as inevitable. This means that the study of management must include an analysis not only of what those choices imply but also what they should imply. The study of management has to be placed in its political and cultural context.

There are three local European historical events in the 1980s which suggest an urgent need for reconsidering the basis for reconstructing management and managerial systems. First, in the United Kingdom, there is a national initiative to establish a comprehensive qualification system for managers based on achieving educational awards, such as a diploma or an MBA. This is seen as leading to the acceptance of managers in posts only if they are 'chartered' by possessing such qualifications. This approach is married to the concept of increasing the differential rewards for managers over specialist technical staff particularly by the use of performance related pay and bonuses. Such an approach, if successful, could create a more distinct managerial élite with the obvious risk that motivation for non-managerial staff could be threatened. The acceptance of this approach raises the issue of access to management training and careers and also that of the acceptance of such a new élite by their subordinates.

Secondly, in Sweden, the Employers' Confederation (SAF) has, over the last five years, been stimulating research into the styles of leadership for top management in Sweden, raising the question of how such Scandinavian management should be fostered. The search for new policies and structures starts from a Swedish as well as from an international perspective. It is based on the analysis of the changing nature of the economic structure of Sweden, both in terms of products, services and new consumption groups. The fostering of such a research programme is directly related to thinking among Swedish politicians, industrialists, civil servants and professionals about future options for Sweden as an independent state. Concepts of management are here directly related to political goals.

Thirdly, as referred to above, the possibilities for European Union and the progress of the Single European Market, ultimately, directly challenge the thinking behind such national managerial initiatives. If managers and professionals are to have the freedom to move across national boundaries in search of work, and if companies are to be encouraged to develop trans-European organizations then European-wide education and training systems are required. A move to an open market across Europe challenges every traditional assumption about managerial roles and behaviour in every member state. It also challenges such assumptions in states like Sweden which are so interconnected with the European Community.

This book therefore is about the future and not the past. It assumes that detailed knowledge of existing systems and their differences is useful – but only in the short run. If things are on the move, then it is prudent to analyze such changes, but also to look to possible patterns for the future which may provide a model and a source of hope.

Keith Thurley and Hans Wirdenius
February 1989

Summary of the argument

Management practices, structures and policies clearly vary considerably between firms, industries and countries; what is less often realized is that the meaning of management itself – the concepts used, assumptions implied in the authority exercised and the objectives pursued – is not universal, although this is assumed to be the case by many practitioners. One reason for this is the domination of American managerial theory throughout the world, although this is now challenged by the 'Japanese management' school. It is argued here that the emergence of the Single European Market (1992) and its consequent changes provides an opportunity to define a distinct European approach to management which could help to spearhead the structural organizational changes necessary to improve the competitive power of the economies of European countries. This will not be easy to achieve as there is a profound sense of pessimism over the future of European society among many European intellectual and cultural leaders. The main need is to overcome the ambiguity over the role of managers in European society. Without this, effective organizational changes can hardly take place. Such ambiguity is not solved by consultants; nor is it likely to be solved by the wholesale acceptance of American 'enterprise culture' or Japanese type company commitment.

The starting point for a European approach is a realistic assessment of actual managerial practice in all three critical levels of organizational behaviour: running and controlling production systems (supervisory management), steering and coordinating 'business units' (operational management) and leading and designing strategic initiatives (enterprise management). Such 'knowledge in use' has to be integrated with a social scientific understanding of management, organizational behaviour and strategic approaches to the planning of change. Four types of change strategies are needed to build a framework for planning change. Essentially the problem of designing effective change strategies depends on the judgement of how to combine such strategies (based on power, expert methodology, research, and project group experimentation) together in the right sequence and how to evaluate such initiatives to learn from mistakes and improve effectiveness, step by step.

The design of change strategies at the enterprise level implies developing the capacity for strategic choice between continuous incremental changes, regeneration programmes and the design of completely new systems. The model of change strategy proposed starts from the search for new objectives and includes the development of a broader vision for the future of the enterprise. The deepening of involvement for all levels of staff has to be pursued, alongside setting new standards of performance and developing new products and services. Eventually there will have to be major changes in work organization and a new reliance on 'built-in' evaluation processes to assess degrees of success and failure. A case study from a Swedish construction firm illustrates this approach and shows the crucial role of the chief executive in initiating change.

No strategic change will be effective, however, unless operational and supervisory management are deeply involved in supporting the change programme. The neglect of supervisory management is one key to declining European organizational effectiveness. This is rooted in the traditional social structure of European societies; candidates for higher management graduating from universities and business schools keep away from too much involvement in the steering of production systems. Unless this is reversed, the supervisory management level will continue to be defined as a lower status routine operation not suitable for the most able and creative managers. Improving production system effectiveness means improving control over input specifications (input efficiency), specifying and controlling throughput (system efficiency), and specifying and controlling output standards (output efficiency). Compared with the human relations, socio-technical systems and organizational development approaches, the total control movement has been the most advanced in tackling such problems of system performance. A case study of failure to change a supervisory system from an OD initiative is given to illustrate the importance of attempting organizational changes rather than simply attempting to change attitudes. Such changes will have to vary according to production system requirements.

A suggested model approach to change at the supervisory management level starts with the identification of production system malfunctions and utilizes supervisory group projects and experimentation as well as 'third-party' research and consultancy to arrive at a complete diagnosis. Changes to the system design will then require 'political' action, preferably by negotiation, and after objectives have been set, the new system can be developed and training and self-development programmes started to improve the skills and knowledge of the supervisors for running the new system. Evaluation processes should be 'built-in' from the beginning. Such a process of change will vary according to whether manufacturing, service or R&D type production systems are involved. What is essential is that supervisory managers and other employees clearly participate in steering the whole process.

The urgency for developing a European management approach rests on the judgement that there is a long-term structural decay in the viability of management within European firms. This is a crucial weakness in meeting the challenge of increasing Japanese and American competition, particularly through direct investment projects. The traditional élite systems of management cannot solve chronic problems of lack of organizational integration due to fragmentation of loyalties and interests by specialist function, status level and geographical location. It is difficult for them to stimulate organizational learning or to utilize fully the talent within the firm that is available.

Two fundamental dimensions of policy choice can be presented in this situation. The first concerns the extent to which 'pluralism' (the recognition of interest group objectives) is accepted and the second refers to the extent to which system integration can be achieved. Both goals are necessary for European management. The Single Market will provide opportunities and necessities for a range of changes of business strategy, from changing the mix of the home market portfolio to the setting up of European level organizations to develop new products and services. To exploit such business opportunities to the full, European management has to combine scientific and rational thinking with pragmatic solutions, the utilization of new ideas with employee commitment and support for creative learning. Only under such conditions will management achieve real legitimacy. Legitimacy for management allows strategic change to take place.

For the individual manager, European management means a requirement to pursue a wide variety of roles at different stages of a career. Such roles will be found partly through internal job

xiv TOWARDS EUROPEAN MANAGEMENT

mobility and partly through changing employers. A balance has to be struck between corporate objectives, social and political objectives and personal and individual goals. Only in this context can a full commitment of employees to change strategies be demanded.

1 The meaning of 'European management'

1.1 A starting point

In his classic film comedy of the 1950s, *Jour de Fête*, Jaques Tati played the part of a French postman in a small village who was so impressed with a film of the super-efficient American postal service that he tried his own way of speeding up deliveries. The joke lay in the incongruity between the traditional French style of living and the postman putting speed and efficiency above all else.

In retrospect, it can be argued that this film went to the heart of the European response to the world situation which followed the end of hostilities in 1945. American influence has been profound. The decisive importance of American military power in ending World War II, the crucial aid given through the Marshall Programme, the nuclear protection against communist military domination, the attraction of a free democratic society combined with high economic efficiency were plain to see. American films and TV programmes were so popular everywhere that governments allowed free access. Mass consumption styles – MacDonalds, Levi jeans, Coca-Cola, etc. – and rock and pop music have spread in popularity among the young even further, across the Iron Curtain, long before the new world of Glasnost. And yet there is another side to the rapid acceptance of American culture and American ways of behaving. Voices – often reactionary in tone – are heard, criticizing the loss of the old ways of living. Political radicals and conservatives point out, with some relish, the flaws in a society in which Kennedy was assassinated, blacks meet so much discrimination and where *Dallas* and *Miami Vice* are such 'role models'. Innovators tend to respond to American ideas by claiming that their own proposals are different and unique.

All these tendencies can be found in the world of management and managerial ideas. Although Europe can claim to be the source of much of what is labelled 'classical theory' in management studies

1

(Fayol, Urwick and, of course, Max Weber could be quoted), it is American management theory – scientific management, human relations, quality control, etc. – which has dominated management teaching in European universities and business schools in recent years. American bestsellers on business practice translated into European languages (e.g. Peters and Waterman, 1982) are the books which are most read by the top managements of European firms. American business schools – Harvard, MIT, Stanford and Chicago – are prized as the most valuable mid-career experiences for European executives, and the famous American consulting firms – McKinsey, Arthur Andersen, etc. – hold a large share of the management consulting market in Western European countries.

The reaction to this American influence has been complicated in the last decade by the rise of the Japanese management school and the growth of Japanese direct investments in European countries. Much of this debate, however, has arrived in Europe through the works of American specialists on Japan (Ouchi, 1981; Pascale and Athos, 1980). The typical first response of European managers, like that of Tati's postman, was to read such literature and then try to find an approach which was better and different. However, as European investments in the United States have increased in the late 1980s, so the American orientation of top management is clearly likely to increase.

1.2 Defining 'European management'

Given this situation it is perhaps surprising that – apart from the the stereotypes of national characteristics and sociological studies of careers and of the social origin of managers – there has been little consciousness within European countries of distinct national approaches to 'management'. The most widely read books comparing management between European countries were by an American, David Granick (1962, 1972). If 'British management' or 'German management' meant little, 'European management' meant even less. At the most, it could be claimed that the term 'European management' refers to a sense that 'excellence' in a European context may mean something different from a perceived 'California style' run company.

Exceptions, however, are recent studies published by researchers at FArådet and intended for managers. In one study, based on interviews of Swedish top leaders from large corporations, government authorities, labour market organizations and politics, a Swedish alternative to the generally fostered Japanese leadership model was launched (Edström, Maccoby, Rendahl and Strömberg, 1985). In another series of case studies the researchers portray Swedish management philosophy of today and claim that a 'doctrine shift' is under way in the management of public and private organizations in Sweden (Beckérus and Edström, 1988). A comprehensive analysis of ongoing and future changes of Swedish economic and industrial life, its values and steering has been presented by de Geer and his colleagues (1987).

Another Scandinavian example is Lindkvist (1988) at the Institute of Organization and Industrial Sociology at the Copenhagen School of Economics who puts the question if it is possible to talk about Nordic management. Making an interpretation of historic literature and responses from Nordic researchers he concludes that the Nordic countries have a unique social organization which makes it difficult to export their management practices to other cultures.

For many managers management is a universal science and 'good management' is the same throughout the whole world. If European firms are not acting in a rational way defining their product market portfolio and carrying out the consequent business strategy systematically, then they are not efficient, anymore than they would be in Cincinnati or Houston.

Part of the origin of these ideas arises from the way that international management is taught in business schools as a set of *universalistic* principles which can accommodate local cultural differences. A recent textbook by Steven Globerman (1986) discusses the use of various techniques by which business decisions can take into account political risks and differences in values between societies. These include the use of 'socio-cultural checklists', the Delphi technique (taking opinions of experts), attitude surveys and use of multiple scenarios of possible alternative future states. He argues:

'As noted above, cultural differences do not as a rule prohibit doing business internationally, although they often oblige management to modify the way business is done from region to region. While modifications may be required, to a greater or lesser extent, in virtually all of the international firm's activities, the particular areas that seem to be most affected by cultural differences are the marketing and personnel-relations functions.' (p. 149)

The implications of this approach are clear enough. International companies have to research such local differences thoroughly and then, if necessary, change their marketing policies and their personnel policies to suit local conditions. There is no sense here that the basic assumptions of the firm's management or their objectives might have to be reconsidered in a different society.

The approach followed by the authors is more in line with that of another popular (British) textbook writer, Michael Brooke (1987). He is rightly sceptical about the nature of 'cultural data', especially from questionnaire surveys, and points out that so-called 'national differences' may reflect occupational cultural traditions and the effects of company size and structure. He argues, however, that:

'Little support is found for extreme universalistic assumptions which are apt to produce more problems than are solved, as superficial resemblances are pressed into support for minimizing the cultural differences. Undoubtedly there is much to be learnt by one culture from another in tackling the problems of industrialization, but the universalistic view suggests that the learning is all one way. Who is to say, on currently available evidence, whether the American emphasis on individual responsibility is more effective than the Japanese on group decision-making in either or both countries? Or vice versa?' (pp. 226–227)

In this passage, Brooke shifts the issue away from the problem of demonstrating that cultural differences are important for managers to understand – which he takes as self-evident – to the much more interesting question of how different cultural assumptions may influence management practice and lead to competing models of excellence. This is the question behind our exploration of European management. How far do current and emerging European social, cultural, economic and political aims and objectives lead to a model of management which is distinct from American or Japanese models?

'European management' should therefore be understood to refer *not* to current practice but to a *possible alternative approach*.

1.3 The 1992 campaign

At the time of writing, the European Community is engaged in a major debate about the implementation of the Single European Market scheduled to start in 1992. This involves the abolition of controls on cross-border trade and on the movement of labour and capital throughout the Community. There are three direct implications for managerial roles involved in this development:

(a) There is likely to be a considerable growth in the cross-border operations of many firms involving the establishment of new branches and firms, acquisitions, etc., so that management will involve a great deal of international experience. Companies are already trying to recruit graduates from different countries and special foreign language training programmes are now being discussed.

(b) Mobility for managers and professionals between countries raises the need for European-wide training and education systems. Should new business schools be established? Should European universities establish joint business studies programmes?

(c) The market is likely to result in much greater competition between firms, and managers must expect to experience greater pressures to rationalize and cut costs, whilst at the same time increasing quality of products and improving customer service. Failures of companies may increase and managers may suffer – along with all employees – a loss of job security.

A current study of the European Foundation into the changing roles and functions of lower and middle management has already established that in 43 cases in six countries such trends are already under way (Thurley and Peccei, 1989). The implication is that managers are more and more likely to find their careers through the external labour market, rather than relying on internal promotion routes. This raises the question of managerial qualifications which is the subject of a separate debate in the United Kingdom on the possibility of establishing a 'professional' status for levels of managers by 'chartering' managers through the attainment of diplomas and MBAs (Institute of Personnel Management Fact Sheet No. 12, Dec. 1988).

The 1992 initiative therefore could lead to major shifts in organizational structures of large firms and to much greater uncertainties in career possibilities for managers at different levels. It certainly challenges existing national systems for education and training – and for recruitment and promotion into management positions. It provides the opportunity for a new approach.

1.4 The legacy of cultural pessimism

The speeches of government ministers and European Community enthusiasts expound great optimism over the prospects of the

Single European market. If we turn to writers on the current European scene, there is a very different note of pessimism in the air.

Any understanding of European artistic expression and consciousness in the twentieth century must start from the horrors of two world wars, the experience of Nazi and Stalinist terror and fear of annihilation through atomic devastation. Early in the century, the German lyrical poet, Rainer Maria Rilke (1934) 'captured the deeper meaning of cultural creation in the century ahead in his insistence on loneliness and the loss of certainty as the constituents of the human condition' (Kitromilides, 1981). In literature and in the visual arts, reality was sought within the person rather than from society and the objective order of the world outside. Intellectuals on the Left have seen the discrediting of Marxist revolution and the slow decline of the perceived validity of socialism. What future objectives for society could be seen now as authentically European?

Cultural pessimism can be expressed from a conservative perspective as well as from the disillusioned Left. Corelli Barnett in his brilliant and polemical attack on the reformers and visionaries in wartime Britain in the 1940s (1986) shows how social reformers ignored the evidence of technological decline and of organizational incompetence in manufacture to build a welfare state on sand. Nationalism and ignorance in the ruling class of the impact of a divided social structure and primitive mass educational achievement on organizational performance are the causes of the failure to build a successful New Jerusalem.

A political commentator might argue here that the movement for European unity is based on a strong sense of alienation from the foolishness and disputes of the past. The transformation of Spain in the last decade and the *rapprochement* between France and Germany are no mean achievements. The fading away of the past, however, also leads to a sense of discontinuity with the past. It may be true that 'cosmopolitan humanism' has re-emerged and provides a greater sense of unity of values across the continent than has been seen for many years (Kitromilides, 1981), but distancing from the past can weaken collective identity and make the possibilities for collective action more difficult.

Effective managerial leadership inevitably points to the need for collective achievement but this is impossible in a climate of cynicism and pessimism about broader social and political goals. The success of American and Japanese firms is not unrelated to the survival of a sense of national identity as a continuing success story in both societies. The opportunities of 1992 will not be grasped unless a similar sense of identity and purpose emerges among Europeans. There were some signs in 1988 that the recent rapid progress towards the abolition of borders has begun to create a new excitement and interest in the creation of a new international type of European society but the legacy of pessimism will not disappear overnight. What is clear is that the task of developing a distinct European managerial approach is a crucial part of changing organizational systems and structures to fit this type of society.

1.5 The need for organizational change

The evidence of the need for radical and comprehensive changes in the organization and structures of both public sector and private firms in West European countries has been accumulating for more than twenty years. The account by Michel Crozier (1964) of the French experience of the 'bureaucratic phenomenon' was one of the earliest diagnoses of the causes of organizational stagnation. His study of a major public administrative agency and of a large publicly owned manufacturing firm depicted these organizations as stratified by hierarchy and divided horizontally by specialist occupation and functional tasks. They were characterized by a decision-making system which was prevented from settling fundamental issues by the latent conflict of interest groups. Managers in such systems solved the 'safe' issues and avoided the difficult problems. The organization could not innovate or adopt strategies of change until a crisis arose from an external threat, when decisions were taken at the top and enforced downwards, in the temporary absence of effective opposition. Although such a situation is usually argued to be typical of the public sector, it is actually found in any stable steady-state organization which is insulated from external shock, perhaps by its market share situation.

Up to the second oil-shock recession of 1979/80, there were numerous examples in European countries of such bureaucracies. Most European national cultures are strongly rule bound and socialist/labour movements have reinforced this tendency to search for impersonal rules to avoid personal authority. Personnel management departments have tended to support such an administrative approach. Middle managers, in particular, suffering lack of promotion in mid-career, may use such rules to avoid risk-taking and the taking on of a heavy workload. Professional groups, entrenched in specialist departments, have also protected their position through insistence on rules governing demarcation of tasks. Hospital systems are excellent examples of this tendency.

Crozier argued that French society was especially prone to develop such organizations. It combined individualism with a class structure that emphasized status distance and the recruitment of top management through a highly selective system of vocational professional schools (*Grandes Écoles*). Strong egalitarian cultures, such as in Scandinavia, also reinforce the tendency to impose general rules on all managers.

British examples of the Crozier type 'bureaucratic phenomena' can certainly be found, but in engineering and many traditional craft based industries – chemical and pharmaceuticals are very different – a second type of organizational malfunction appears to be widespread. The elements of this type of organizational situation were analysed in depth by an outstanding study of the electronics industry by Tom Burns and George Stalker in 1961. Here there were many examples given of formally hierarchical organizations, which, under the pressures of attempts to develop new products, were locked into incoherent and fragmented conflicts between specialist functions, sales, development teams, production departments, research laboratories, etc. Communications between departments and operational staff and senior management were frequently difficult, not because of status distance but because of the conflicting political games being played around career systems and the interests of specialists in particular projects. The track record of the wartime UK electronics industry and its failure to deliver products on time is also discussed by Barnett (1986). Unreliable delivery dates, poor quality components and rising cost ratios and wastage figures indicate a failure of middle managers to establish adequate control systems. One effect in high technology industry is a massive underutilization of human talent – through stalled projects, the hoarding of expert staff for future projects, etc. – and this is currently being explored as part of a study on the roles and development needs of electronic engineers (Thurley, Lam and Lorriman, 1988).

A third type of organizational problem has enjoyed more public exposure: the failure of firms to avoid continuous industrial relations disputes, particularly of a wildcat nature. There are, of course, many causes of disputes, and poor industrial relations have created a large loss of man days from production only in certain industries, certain firms and in certain European countries. In general terms, however, the growth of shop steward organizations in large manufacturing, transport and service sector firms in the 1960s and 1970s – especially in UK, Ireland and Italy – reflected a collapse of lower and middle management status and authority and a power game between labour union committees and enterprise management. It is relevant to point out that this situation did not occur to the same extent in countries with formally established works councils and co-determination (Sweden, the Netherlands and West Germany) although France, for specific reasons, is a deviant case.

The first and third type of organizational problem prompted the Conservative government in the UK since 1979 to move towards a market economy by privatizing public enterprises and bringing in legislation to allow employers to sue trade unions for actions beyond a narrow definition of a trade dispute. Unemployment and tighter legal control has greatly reduced strikes. Competition, of a limited nature, has not had a similar effect yet on the incidence of the bureaucratic phenomena in the newly privatized public services. The 'enterprise culture' – the sponsorship of small and medium firms into undertaking new ventures – similarly does very little to solve the internal organizational problems of would-be innovative firms.

1.6 The 'Company Doctor' solution

According to a recent study of corporate profitability levels in publicly quoted companies in the UK (Slatter, 1984), 20% were in trouble in the sense that net profit ratios, measured at constant prices to eliminate the effects of inflation, had declined for three or more years. This study examined accounts over a 15 year period. If a recovery or 'turn-around' situation is measured by the fact that companies in trouble consequently increased their profit ratios in four of the following six years, then Slatter argued, 25% of the ailing companies had been successfully 'turned around'.

This figure of one in five companies at any time being at risk of collapse is argued by Kharbanda and Stallworthy (1987) as being generally true and supported by other evidence. They then argue the case for the 'company doctor', the use of a top manager who is introduced to rationalize and cut costs, develop more profitable business and stimulate managers and employees to accept drastic changes in their methods and working relationships. Sir John Cuckney, Ian Macgregor and Umeo Oyama in Japan (Hann, 1985) are given, among others, as examples.

It is clearly possible for a ruthless rationalization policy to produce better financial results for one company. There are many examples in Europe in the 1980s, where out of date factories have been shut, obsolete products scrapped and business has been concentrated on existing profitable lines or new and expanding services. The difficulty comes in seeing this as a general and long-term answer to the problem of modernizing and improving the performance of European economies. There are three reasons for this difficulty.

First, it is obvious that such a policy ignores the costs to local communities in terms of unemployment and the downward cycle of recession for subcontractors and smaller firms indirectly affected by the shutting of plants. Although job creation policies and retraining can help in such circumstances, in several parts of the European Community experience has shown that this requires political mobilization of the local community, the support of the labour movement, the help of banks and regional funds, etc. These are social costs which do not show in the balance sheet of the firm being 'doctored'. They have to be met and political constraints on rationalization policies are therefore inevitable in most countries.

A second problem with the 'company doctor' solution is the rather simple individualism assumed in the concept. Although the role of the chief executive is crucial (see Chapter Six), an essentially 'political' solution (based on imposed decisions) requires very strong support, for example from institutional shareholders, *and* as Crozier argued, an essentially temporary crisis situation to silence the opposition. The Great Man theory works best for short-term battles, not for long wars.

Thirdly, and most important, the long-term survival of European society can be argued to depend on its capacity to develop new products and services from an advanced level of science and technology. If Japanese industry has been able to wipe out key industries in Europe, such as motor cycle and camera producers, this is because of its capacity to link R&D, product development, effective production engineering, subcontracting policies and the 'positioning' of products at the right time in certain market segments (Kotler, Fahey and Jatusripitak, 1985). Such success requires a heavy investment in research and development and considerable collaboration between firms, with public support. It is very unlikely that corporate rationalization policies can allow European companies alone to compete with such an approach. It is all too likely that, as in the Westland affair, it simply leads to foreign control over European companies.

1.7 A general diagnosis

The position of management in Western Europe is the key to economic revival and needs a general diagnosis.

There is as yet no generally accepted ideology or model of European management which can be set against that of Japanese or American management. This issue is central to this book. Social and cultural diversity is a great strength in Western Europe, but it is a difficulty when when it comes to global ideological competition. The need to evolve such a model is crucial for tackling the problem of declining managerial legitimacy.

Traditional ideas on 'management' developed in Europe in the nineteenth century come from four major sources:

(*a*) Lower and middle managers in industry tended to be promoted from supervisors, foremen or Meister who were the heads of specialist tradesmen occupational groups in workshops.

(*b*) Administrative and commercial managers were recruited from clerical workers who themselves entered the companies from grammar schools or gymnasia.

(*c*) Entrepreneurs and capitalists who owned enterprises owed their authority to their property and not to their 'managerial' expertise. Family-based top management continued to be important in all European countries into the twentieth century.

(*d*) Educational élites were produced through special vocational schools (*cadres*) in France or through the universities (e.g. in Germany and Italy). Such élites owed their authority to their technical knowledge and their educational status. They rose to top management in such countries.

In the twentieth century, the advent of American scientific management established the authority of managers based on their organizational expertise to solve work problems. This had considerable effect in Germany and Scandinavia but it failed for many years to establish a professional managerial class based on this principle alone. The growth of universities since the Second World War, however, provided a much greater flow of graduates as a basis for management careers. Such graduates sometimes entered companies through general trainee schemes, but in the UK particularly, the importance of the professional institutes encouraged:

(e) Specialist careers and qualifications for engineers, accountants, personnel managers, etc., educated through universities and higher educational institutions.

Business schools have been generally slow to expand until the last decade, but it should be noted that:

(f) In Scandinavia and the Netherlands, schools of economics have provided business education for an élite for many years as a qualification system for higher management.

The result is that European 'managers' had a profoundly ambiguous status and identity. As mass education expanded in the post second-war period, so the position of the traditional élites has declined. In some countries, the growth of the financial services sector and the high rewards for participants has undercut the attraction of specialist technical and professional training for a managerial career.

André Laurent (1985) recently compared the extent to which the national origin of managers affects their views of what proper management should be about. His questionnaire analysis applied to upper middle level managers on executive programmes at INSEAD in Fontainebleau (a European business school) but was also tested on samples in two multinationals. From the study, four indices and clusters of attitude were distinguished:

(a) Management as a 'political role';
(b) Management as an authority position;
(c) Management as a formal organizational role (function based);
(d) Management as a position in a hierarchy.

In Table 1.1 the average index scores are given for countries ranged in different groups. The table shows a very different pattern of role perceptions in the various groups of countries. Probably the most striking conclusion is the contrast between the 'Latin' countries which score high on all indices and some 'Northern' countries which seem to show a much more specialized and limited concept of management.

Another way of showing such contrasts is to consider the type of position identity which can be encompassed in a managerial position. Figure 1.1 illustrates some of the more important identities. Confusions in role identity relate to values and loyalty and affect the capacity of managers to co-operate closely.

	n	Political role	Authority position	Organizational position and functional role	Hierarchical position
Percentage of members perceiving management as:					
	v				
Italy	32	66	61	84	66
France	219	62	65	81	50
Belgium	45	–	61	81	50
West Germany	72	36	34	85	47
Switzerland	63	51	32	85	43
Denmark	54	26	46	80	37
Great Britain	190	32	48	80	37
Netherlands	42	36	49	67	33
Sweden	50	42	46	57	25
USA	50	43	30	66	28

Source: Laurent (1985).

Table 1.1 *Conceptions of the managerial role by managers from different national origin: percentages of national samples classified according to four indices.*

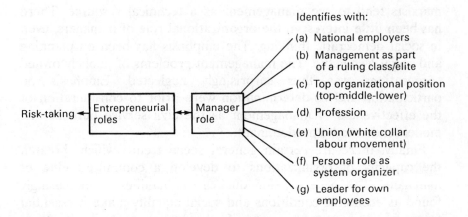

Figure 1.1 *Ambiguities in management identities.*

In general terms the social basis for building a legitimate managerial élite is difficult in societies originally based on a clear class structure but now in confused transient state towards a mass society. Dahrendorf (1959) believed that bureaucratic or organizational position would replace social class positions based on occupational strata, but this has not happened except as a temporary phenomenon. Management may retain an expert status in societies as West Germany or Sweden, but it is difficult to do this in societies such as the United Kingdom, where there was a variety of routes into management and internal promotion was of great importance. In many types of organizations it would be fair to argue that there was no concept of management as such. These included public administration, voluntary bodies and professionally dominated organizations such as hospitals.

All traditional routes into management are under change and new types of managers, especially those with American MBAs, are entering the field. The new business schools are also attempting to build a new type of élite. What should be noted is that the position of those who have not been lucky enough to participate in selective education is difficult and this makes the social solidarity of management difficult to achieve.

Some large organizations, particularly in the public sector, have found that their lower managers have become unionized, usually through white-collar unions. These unions tend to emphasize the difference in interest between lower and top management. Socialist thinking towards management has indeed been highly ambiguous. Under capitalism, marxists believe that managers are 'agents of capital' and should be resisted (or infiltrated). Under socialism, marxists tend to see management as a technical resource. There has been little interest in the organizational role of managers, even in social democratic thinking. The emphasis has been on planning and social ownership. The management problems of publicly owned corporations was thus surprisingly neglected. Emphasis on participation and co-determination were prior to consideration of the effectiveness of management as the civil service bureaucratic model tended to be predominant.

Finally, there are certain general social trends which threaten the capacity of organizations to develop a committed élite of managers. The necessity for dual-career families is increasingly found as economic conditions and social equality make it essential for women to have work careers. Such dual-career family situations increasingly prevent geographical mobility and the type of work commitment found in Japanese companies, at least in Japan. The growth of a leisure culture and the strong values of private life separated from the field of work could easily lead to managers in midcareer restricting their work commitments and settling for a modest career in middle management. European holidays are a vivid example of this trend. It is difficult to envisage American, Japanese or Korean managers planning their six week summer vacation.

The results of these trends are relatively easy to see. It is difficult in European companies to mobilize the talents of their managers and employees to meet the threats of international competition. There are by now many warning voices and the prophets of decline and fall are making themselves heard. The reactions of Europeans to these warnings has been slow and the savage criticisms of European management found in some American and Japanese political circles are not difficult to explain.

2 The age of the guru: chasing after straws

2.1 The American invasions

Europeans have recognized American expertise in management for nearly a hundred years. In the early 1950s the flow of American ideas into European firms was greatly stimulated by the Marshall Plan project activities. Numerous joint working parties from unions and management travelled to see the latest systems and the European Productivity Movement (EPA) held several conferences with American speakers.

The 1960s saw the beginnings of American business consultancy in Western European societies. Step by step, large American consulting firms such as McKinseys increased their market share. Famous academics such as Dick Beckard, Blake and Mouton, Ed Schein, Harold Leavitt and Warner Bennis began to appear regularly at company seminars, professional management experts such as Peter Drucker and Saul Gellerman were the stars of management conferences, and Emersons, McKinsey and Arthur Young were hired by governments and companies to restore health to their ailing organizations. The penetration of American ideas was of course very uneven. Sweden, the Netherlands, West Germany, the United Kingdom and Ireland were the most affected, and France and other Mediterranean and central European countries such as Austria the most resistent. Comparisons between Japan and Western European countries in this period would show a significant difference in the response of managers and academics to the American managerial gospel. The Japanese made the most thorough studies of American methods in complete detail and attempted to replicate the programmes in Japan, modifying when necessary. The volume and scope of Japanese interest in American management was astonishing. As we now know, the whole basis of so-called 'Japanese management', especially as applied to production planning, quality control, inventory control, etc., was developed in the 1950s and 1960s by importing American ideas and methods and integrating these with more indigenous systems (e.g. *nenko joritsu* or seniority systems). Some European companies were also interested in these ideas, and some became involved in systematic change projects as with the OD experiments in ICI, Shell, etc. Generally, however, there was no widespread replication of American systems, except where American consultants installed such systems. In reality, European management was much more resistant to American ideas than Japanese managers, even in countries where American influence appeared to be at its greatest.

The latest wave of American ideas on management started in 1983 with the European publication of Peters and Waterman's classic, *In Search of Excellence*. According to Christopher Lorenz *(Financial Times*, July 2, 1986), *Excellence* had sold 100,000 copies in France in these years, higher numbers in West Germany and the UK, and more than 30,000 per country in Spain, Sweden and the Netherlands. The significance of the *Excellence* book lies with the fact that it signals a clear break with the traditional model of an 'M-form organization' based on divisions and profit centres, which was part of the central message of consultancy firms such as McKinseys since the 1960s. *Excellence* argues the case for strong corporate leadership based on a distinct company culture and the importance of identity and motivation over control systems. It is highly significant that it has spearheaded a wave of interest among French managers in American ideas. Lorenz quotes Gerard Thulliez, the senior consultant of McKinseys in France: 'There is a greater willingness to treat business as something respectable and essential to the life of the country. There is also more readiness to learn lessons from others, instead of making judgments about them, which is the neutral tendency of our civilization' *(Financial Times*, July 2, 1986).

According to Wilhelm Rall, the equivalent of Thulliez in West Germany, in Germany there is 'a new feeling of insecurity about what are the right management methods to apply. In the past, when everyone was successful, there was no need for external role models like Iacocca (Iacocca – *An American Career*). Now there most definitely is.' He goes on to admit, however, that 'We've always been more ready than the British and the French to look for external role models and to transfer American ideas' *(Financial Times*, July 2, 1986).

It is important to note, says Lorenz, that there are remarkably few bestselling books on business that are written by European authors. One main reason appears to be that 'the really influential management gurus (in Europe) prefer not to reveal their knowledge in books' (Dr Eberhard Möstl of Moderne Industrie, quoted by Lorenz). Managers have traditionally not looked to books for the basis of their knowledge. This again contrasts with Japan where more than ten million copies of books on Taylorism and scientific management were frequently sold in the second and third decade of this century.

One clear theme of recent management literature is concentration on the methods of the successful business leader. It is difficult to do this in societies where such figures are frequently discredited in the media and easier, by contrast, to discuss American leaders and their expertise.

2.2 Why are there management gurus?

The question needs to be asked as to why the *Excellence* literature has been so popular. What needs are being addressed?

It is, of course, difficult to be precise in answering such questions and there is a temptation to fall back on stereotyped notions of media manipulation, the power of advertising and the role of the American consultancy and publishing firms who need a product and image to sell. Behind these phenomena, however, it is possible to distinguish the evidence of needs perceived by top management of companies for projecting simple and clear ideas on the objectives of the company and the philosophy of the board in following such objectives.

The last chapter referred to the argument that European managers needed to be persuaded to take a more 'strategic' approach (and to be less concerned with local problem–solving and survival in the short run). Such emphasis on 'strategic management' is commonplace in business school teaching and it lays the ground for thinking about the need for a set of criteria by which boards of directors could evaluate alternative policies and decide on a clear course of action. A 'management guru' or a 'packaged' set of principles and statements are often very useful for giving legitimacy to these strategic choices. Managers need support for their policy choices and in European society there has been considerable distance between business leaders and intellectual leaders in the universities and professions. The guru phenomenon, in a word, is a response to the vacuum in intellectual debate on business policy. Managers and businessmen can look to their own prophets and ignore the academic theorists and philosophers who seem at best disinterested in business and at worst positively hostile to business and managerial objectives. (See Kenneth Blanchard and Spencer Johnson's *The One-Minute Manager* (1982).)

2.3 American management versus Japanese management

Many of these management ideas have intrinsic merit but the problem lies with the way that companies look at them for quick solutions. The ideas that have been most potent in challenging the dominance of American ideas in management, however, are those labelled 'Japanese management'. There is an overlap with several of the American concepts as much has been learnt by the Japanese from American theorists and American companies. It is useful here, however, to summarize the debate between American and Japanese approaches in polar opposites. This at least points to the different emphases in the two approaches.

American management

American management theory is built on seven crucial ideas:

1. *Scientific management.* Using a systematic approach to improve task performance.
2. *Classical management theory.* Defining roles in terms of specific job/role responsibilities and authority.
3. *Individualism.* Assuming that managers are primarily individuals with their own personalities and interests and their own concept of individual self-interest.
4. *Human relations.* Concern for fostering work group norms and relationships to serve organizational goals.
5. *Contingency theory.* All organizations need to develop structures and policies which are relevant for the particular context of the particular organization. All organizations therefore should be different.
6. *Planned organizational change.* Change requires a systematic approach to change organizational structures and culture.
7. *Strategic choice management.* Organizations should try to define the basic business strategies required to achieve a satisfactory market position. This then leads to designing structures that fit this strategy.

Japanese management

Japanese management is essentially in contrast an argument for equality as the basis of competition and co-operation. This rejects the implicit technocratic approach of American scientific management. There are also seven crucial ideas which summarize the approach:

1. *Collective responsibility.* All members of an organization should feel responsibility for the success of that organization.
2. *Generalist roles and job rotation.* All employees work for the organization and should be trained to perform a wide variety of roles. They do not own their jobs – they may have to do anything and need training for this.
3. *Trust of subordinates.* Subordinates need to be allowed to get on with their work. They have potential which should be stimulated.
4. *Protection of all employees.* All employees are vulnerable and need protection whilst working for the organization.
5. *Life careers should be planned.* Individuals need to perceive their whole potential career as an opportunity which offers a challenge for them to develop their skills and knowledge.
6. *Pragmatic adaption and rationalism.* Everything changes, so management must be flexible enough to change to new circumstances.
7. *Identity with the 'michi' ('the way') and personal work colleagues.* The work ethic is seen as a daily personal experience and is essentially derived from constant interactions with others in the work group. Employees therefore need to have a clear identity with the way they live in the organization and to show affection and loyalty to their co-workers.

Essentially the debate between American and Japanese theorists takes place around these four issues:

(*a*) Work security versus individual freedom.
(*b*) Organizational loyalty versus job competence.
(*c*) Consultation and involvement versus management authority.
(*d*) Work group innovation versus specialist know-how.

Japanese management therefore leads to emphasis on building organizational commitment and enforcing tight controls over individual behaviour. (Discipline on such issues as absenteeism and smoking is often severe.)

European managers may find this debate to be less than useful. One can find both collective responsibility and individualistic behaviour in European firms. It is also clear that such Japanese ideas are easier to develop in a 'green-field' factory than in a bank or securities house. The former offers an opportunity to develop a whole and relatively autonomous system afresh and the latter are constrained by centralized control from the head office (Takamiya and Thurley, 1985). Critics in Europe often point to the inflexibility of the Japanese firm in its hierarchy and to the lack of consideration for individuals with their own private responsibilities. The socialist left will also point to the hostility to 'independent' trade unions. In the UK a compromise approach of a 'single union agreement' has been pioneered in Japanese electronics companies, but this has not prevented many Japanese firms recently trying to establish a non-union shop (Basset, 1987). More importantly, this debate does not solve the structural problems of European organization – the lack of integration – and it does little to solve the crisis of European managers in search of a distinct identity and approval.

2.4 Demand for quick-fix solutions

European managers are not only apparently interested in American business heroes and business gurus, there is also a steady demand for immediate solutions to problems bought 'off the shelf'. These are available usually through consultants and they include the following at present.

New reward systems for managers and key employees

Two ideas are prevalent at the moment:

(a) Greater individual financial rewards related to managerial performance (measured by agreed performance indicators). These are usually bonuses or share option schemes.

(b) Greater involvement of managers and key employees in the ownership of the business and in the sharing of risk. This takes the form of 'management buy-out' schemes and the offer of share options. Good examples are that of Premier Foods, the ex Food Division of Cadbury-Schweppes, in the UK and that of Volvo in Sweden.

In both cases the argument is that motivation will be enhanced by relating the performance of the company to actual individual rewards and capital holdings.

The quality standards movements

Specific ideas include quality circles, 'total quality control', zero defects, etc. All these methods involve attempts to mobilize employee involvement in the setting and policing of quality standards and in thinking of improvements in methods, the reduction of waste, etc. The use of small project groups or circles are most frequent.

Tighter production control standards

The 'just in time' (Kanban) system from Toyota which synchronizes the flow of subcontracted components for final assembly is argued to be useful to reduce inventory costs. There is also a new interest in Japanese production engineering, in the importance of simplified factory layout and the use of flexible manufacturing systems (FMS) – computer controlled machine tools grouped into 'production cells'. Such systems allow radical changes to be introduced in shop-floor production system design.

Work restructuring

In a small minority of companies experiments are still being carried out in restructuring work organization to increase the range of tasks for workers and changing the nature of supervisory control.

Service management courses ('charm courses')

In Scandinavia, particularly, these have been of considerable importance, especially in airlines (SAS, British Airways,) hotels, service operations (e.g. the Post Office in Denmark), etc. The idea is to provide mass training of all staff in basic customer service attitudes and behaviour.

Assessment centres

Large companies in particular have invested in centres for locating potential talent in their staff using batteries of tests, interviews and exercises.

Head hunting and 'out-posting'

Consultants are used to recruit senior management and to find jobs for them when they are no longer seen as useful.

Single union agreements

The rapid development of Japanese and other foreign investment in new factories in Europe, particularly in green-field sites, is associated with a movement to simplify industrial relations by negotiating a single agreement with single status, built-in consultative processes and arbitration to avoid strikes and any type of industrial action. Such agreements have been particularly important in the United Kingdom (Basset, 1987; Trevor, 1988).

2.5 Skill at adapting new ideas

What is the effect on managerial performance of living in a world bombarded by a constant barrage of new ideas and possible new techniques? Young management trainees are constantly reminded that it is their role to be continuously innovative. Specialists try to persuade others in different functions of the importance of the latest improvements in their own field of knowledge. But how many such innovations actually live up to the promises declared by the innovator? Short-term effects obviously occur and consultants and managers can claim success for their schemes. Long-term and comprehensive evaluation of managerial innovations rarely take place and if they do they are frequently pessimistic. (Examples here include QWL programmes, the effect on morale of share ownership schemes and office automation systems.)

The gap between the optimism of the innovator and the pessimism of the evaluator is no accident. One clear reason for this is the process by which such innovation takes place. Frequently, the start is the interest generated by the apparent success of the new idea in other organizations. The managerial innovator then tries to persuade his organization to adopt the new policy, technique or approach. Experiments may lead to large-scale implementation. Essentially this is an *ad hoc* approach focusing on the new idea as a solution to a particular problem. What is neglected are the indirect effects of the innovation on the whole system and the scepticism of other managers and specialists on the value of the experiment. There are numerous examples in Europe of managers who enthusiastically try out new ideas but neglect the skills required to achieve a consensus behind the innovation.

This lack of skill may be rooted in the educational process. Business schools and universities develop analytical thinking and cognitive frames of reference. Case studies are analysed in terms of strategic choices. The problem of implementing such choices receives far less attention. To do this would require simulation and understanding of the 'political' organizational difficulties facing the innovator.

At a personal level, there is frequently little understanding of the behaviour and values required by managers to persuade others to change. In European societies, managers frequently still behave as an élite and the social distance proclaimed by their personal behaviour to others – which is so important for their identity – is a cause of hidden scepticism by their subordinates or colleagues.

The age of the guru, therefore, is an age of false promises. Exciting new ideas turn into disappointment. For every new management message, there are sceptics waiting for it to fail.

3 The study of management practice

3.1 What is a manager?

Economic development and industrialization has taken place at different times and in different ways in the various nation states that make up the area known as Western Europe. In Northern Italy and parts of the Flemish area there was craft manufacture in the latter part of the Medieval period (thirteenth/fourteenth centuries) and in Southern Ireland and parts of Portugal, Spain and Southern Italy, industrialization was not known until the last twenty years (post-1965). Until this century there was no special concept of management used in European languages. In general terms, occupational titles defined identities and positions within the class structure. In the nineteenth century in most European societies family – owned enterprises created a special status and role for the owner and a number of key employee roles for senior and reliable workers. Foremen and supervisors developed a large number of special occupational titles as the subcontracting system declined, and chief clerks were appointed to run the offices of the new enterprises (Pollard, 1965). The American term 'manager', imported at the beginning of this century, was only used at first to describe the roles of the persons in charge of distinct establishments where this was separated from the role of the entrepreneur and of the owner. A typical managerial role in the United Kingdom, by the First World War, was that of the 'works manager' or factory manager.

In 1917, Sidney Webb was trying to define the new occupational group of managers as follows:

'In my opinion, the profession of the manager, under whatever designation, is destined, with the ever-increasing complication of man's enterprises, to develop a steadily increasing technique and a more and more specialized vocational training of its own.' (Webb, 1917)

Scientific management literature from Taylor, Gilbreth, Rowen and others was essentially devoted to trying to improve the effectiveness of persons in these roles. A second and complementary type of literature from Fayol to Chester Barnard was devoted to clarifying the role of the chief executive in charge of enterprises and was therefore much broader in scope.

The Second World War brought many changes in this situation. First, a whole new literature on the foreman or supervisor was created, drawing both on scientific management and the new leadership theories of the human relations movement. Supervisors were said to be 'part of management' although they frequently commented that they could not see that they were treated as such by the owners of enterprises. Secondly, management associations were created, especially in the United Kingdom to further the training and development of 'managers' on a professional association model. More important was the implicit widening of the term 'manager' or management to include all levels in an organization that had responsibility for the running of units. Civil servants, nursing sisters in hospitals, headmasters of schools, etc., were all encouraged to see themselves as the 'managers' of their organizations or units. Probably of the greatest importance, however, was the development of American-type 'business management' education in the universities and business schools.

Two major American–type business schools were founded in the UK in the 1960s and international schools developed in France and Switzerland. This development in turn stimulated the development of concepts and theories which were focused on the problem of improving the direction of enterprises. Concepts of business strategy were taught to help the staff at corporate level to take a more rational and systematic view of business policy. Management teaching was focused on the policy choices facing company planners and the board members themselves. Confusion was implicit in the use of the term 'manager' to cover so many levels within the organization, who were also dealing with many different types of problems.

3.2 The failure of empirical research on managerial roles

In the period since 1950 there have been a number of abortive attempts to study managerial roles directly. Carlson (1951) started by studying entrepreneurial or board level roles and in the UK there were studies of managers' work activities by observation, interview and questionnaire by Stewart (1967), Burns (1957), Lupton and Horne (1963) and others. They revealed a bewildering range of work roles and activities as was also discovered by Sayles (1964) and Mintzberg (1973) in the United States. None of these studies produced any really satisfactory conceptualization of managerial work as they were unable to place the role activity in a model of organizational behaviour.

It is noteworthy that most of this work (Mintzberg is an exception) was ignored by the business schools (Sayles, 1964). The important issues there were business policy and types of control system. Organizational behaviour was taught in terms of models, concepts and theories usually separate from this discussion of business policy. Supervisory management problems exercised the interest of the specialist foreman training institutes (for example in Scandinavia) and the technical schools, but disappeared from the agenda of the business schools. The problems of the works manager were also not discussed as the crucial issues were perceived to lie in enterprise business policy. Techniques were developed and discussed for use by specialist functional management (for example discounted cash flow (DCF)) but this did not involve the analysis of managerial role problems.

By the 1980s, therefore, attention was being more and more focused on enterprise policy and governmental policies which affected business decisions. Social science research focused on such issues, and although the term 'management' was used constantly apart from the continuing work of Rosemary Stewart and Henry Mintzberg, there was little empirical research or theory related to the actual roles of managers at different levels. In this situation managers in their professional associations were well aware of the irrelevance of such academic research to their actual problems – and frequently made this point. The study of actual management practice is still a largely unexplored area except for case study evidence and personal experience.

It can be argued that the quality of the vocational training and education for managers has probably been severely limited by the lack of a body of systematic research on management practice.

3.3 A suggested framework: definition of management

Such research requires a systematic framework as a basis for comparative studies. As a first step, we need to redefine management in terms of level and in terms of a system concept rather than role.

The first concept needed is the building block of organizational design, the concept of a 'production system'.

Production system

The concept of a 'production system' refers here to *any specific humans organization which has been set up with a given technology to produces goods or services at a definable level or rate*. (Technology itself is used in the general Woodward sense of 'the collection of plant, machines, tools and recipes available at a given time for the execution of the production task and the rationale underlying their utilization' (1965).)

The idea of a production system is that it is an organization with a definable and planned output. The boundaries of such a system may be difficult to determine in practice, but generally it is identical to the concept of 'socio-technical system' used by Tavistock Institute theorists. It should be noted that the concept covers all types of work situation and not merely manufacturing. A production system can produce maintenance services, marketing services, construct buildings or produce research results. In a company therefore and within a given establishment there may be a number of such systems (See Appendix).

Business unit

An enterprise may be composed of one or a number of business units. A business unit is defined as *a cluster of production systems covering the full range of commercial/production activities which are accounted for separately and discretely as one unit*, e.g. a profit/cost centre or a separately accounted division. The boundaries of the unit are determined by commercial/financial practice.

Supervisory management

The first level of management deals with the supervisory function of a production system. Supervisory managers occupy roles in a 'supervisory system' which 'steers' a production system through three main activities: (a) dealing with individual disturbances to the system, (b) trying to prevent future disturbances, and (c) trying to develop the production system and to redesign it.

Such a supervisory system can therefore be defined as *a social systems consisting of people who are seen as being in continuing control of a production system*, i.e. where the supervisors are recognized to have responsibility for control and where they are actually working together on common problems.

Operational management

Operational management is concerned with the running of business units and as such has the task of co-ordinating and integrating the outputs of the production systems so as to raise the output levels of the business unit. We can define operational management therefore as *a social system consisting of people who are recognized as being in charge of the overall direction of business units*. This is clearly a definition restricted to market-oriented organizations. In public service organizations there may be no clear distinctions between operational and enterprise management and in this case there will be simply production systems (and supervisory management) and enterprise management. Where there is no clear concept of a commercial or accountable unit we are not dealing even with enterprise management but simply levels of enterprise administration.

Enterprise management

Enterprise management deals with the steering of enterprise activities, through policy decision-making, decisions on corporate objectives, priorities and strategies of action. We can define enterprise management therefore as *a social system consisting of people who are recognized as being in charge of the overall direction of the enterprise*. The boundaries of the enterprise may also be difficult to define, but as this is a legal/commercial term, it will be necessary to use strict legal criteria.

It also needs to be emphasized that where enterprises are not divided into clear business units, then there is no clear role for operational management. The reality is that operational management is merged into enterprise management even if it is labelled 'middle management'. Where regional levels exist in a national organization but without being accounted for as a business unit, then they will be treated as enterprise management.

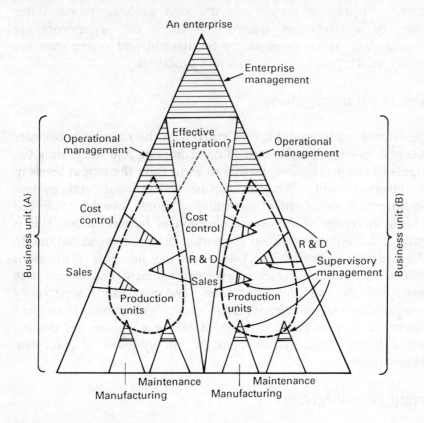

Figure 3.1 *Types of organization system and management*

Figure 3.1 summarizes these differences and distinctions. A clear conceptual framework is necessary for laying the foundations of a 'European' approach. The distinction between types of management is fundamental. It should be borne in mind in considering the usefulness and validity of various managerial theories.

4 The gap in management theory

4.1. Prescription versus analysis

Management theory from Fayol onwards has mainly been prescriptive/normative, setting out principles for managers to follow. Originally, management principles were simply the ideas and experience of top management being set down for others to follow (e.g. Sloan, *My years with General Motors*, (1963)). More recently the tendency has been for consultants and academic entrepreneurs to write out the crucial objectives, techniques, systems and frameworks which they believe managers should adopt and utilize (e.g. Peters and Waterman (1982), Ouchi (1981), Drucker (1955), Gellerman (1968), Blanchard and Johnson (1982), Likert (1961), Urwick and Brech (1947), Humble (1973), Blake and Mouton (1985), Kepner and Tregoe (1965)).

European academic social science tends to reject such a prescriptive literature as illegitimate for two reasons. It is argued that scholarship has to be 'value free', detached and critical rather than biased and normative. Karl Popper, in particular, stresses a model of social science which is concentrated on the testing of hypotheses by the use of independent evidence (1960). Students are taught models and concepts for carrying out strict analytical work using objective data sets as evidence. Accepting prescriptions from others is seen as one step on the road to an authoritarian 'closed society' with a 'party line' for all circumstances.

A second reason is the radical tradition of university-based social science. Managers and businessmen are seen as men of power attempting to extend their influence by setting down prescriptions and norms for others to follow, which in fact protect their own roles and positions. Social scientists argue that they should be allowed to examine such propositions in a critical fashion and to expose the assumptions made by managers and to trace the implications of such policies. The continuing criticism of Taylorism by such social scientists is an excellent example of this tradition.

This conflict between prescription and analysis is found in a more subtle way in business school and management educational literature. There are, of course, a number of functional areas of management where standard texts are still mostly prescriptive. Marketing, accounting and finance and production control are obvious examples. In behavioural science, the purpose of many books is to teach managers what they need to know in order to handle the 'human factor' successfully in their organizations. This is quite explicit in the bestseller *The One-Minute Manager* (Blanchard and Johnson, 1982). Here the guru instructs the novice manager in a manner similar to the first reel of a cinema film portraying a hero learning the martial arts in order to defeat a gang of villains.

In most books and articles in behavioural science, however, analytical frameworks are used and researchers emphasize particular factors, concepts, hypotheses and methods which affect organizational behaviour. Maslow, McGregor, Herzberg, McClelland and Vroom, for example, have all written books and articles to 'explain' the problem of work motivation. The message to managers of how to adapt their own behaviour in order to 'motivate' subordinates is often extremely indirect. Intelligent managers are expected to read these books and then draw their own conclusions as to how their own behaviour should be modified. This is simple if the research findings are presented in terms of dichotomies such as that of McGregor's Theory X and Y. It is also clear (even if the validity can be challenged) in the case of Herzberg. The manager is being exhorted to pursue a policy of job enrichment by deepening the opportunities for his subordinates to increase their intrinsic task satisfaction in performing a wider range of tasks. The reader of Likert should be clear on the supposed superiority of System 4 styles of leadership. Problems, however, arise with more complex 'behavioural science' research, especially where attempts are made to take into account environmental factors that affect the nature of organizational behaviour. The manager may well ask, in these cases, what is the message for him (or her)?

A good example here is the small but growing literature on comparative management which concentrates on the different institutions and values behind management in different countries (e.g. Harbison and Myers (1959), Abegglen (1957), Webber (1969), Weinshall (1977), Graves (1986), Hickson and McClelland (1981), Hofstede (1980), Bettigniez (1969), England (1967), Neghandi (1971), Stam (1982), Rubenowitz (1967)). One problem for this group is the tendency to oversimplify national culture and make comparisons based on exaggerated cultural stereotypes.

Much of the currently popular debate on Japanese management can easily lead to managers accepting that the Japanese are different (and successful) but concluding that 'we're different, so that it is difficult to apply those ideas here'.

In the last twenty years much organizational research has been dominated by the argument that organizational differences reflect the external constraints and opportunities (differences in markets, government legislation, national culture, labour union power, etc.).

This academic emphasis on 'contingency theory' from Woodward and Lawrence and Lorsch has caused a negative effect on the development of management theory, i.e. the emphasis has been on the variations in organizational structure, variations in environment, systems theory, etc., and discussion of the way that individual managerial roles can be played almost disappear in this research (for example in 'socio-technical theory'). Managers still ask for help, and journals are full of articles about new techniques (quality circles, zero defects, total quality control, etc.). The advantage to top management of hiring consultants for specific services against relying on more general management research is that consultant projects can be focused on the specific problems, and the time and activities of the consultant can be directly and completely controlled. In this way there is a tendency for a widening of the gap between 'academic' research and consultancy. The frameworks produced by consultancy agencies are often hardly related to academic models and are frequently clear reflections of top managers' own views of themselves which is in the tradition of Urwick and Sloan. This gap between consultants' prescriptions and academic organization theory has been a major limitation on the value of such frameworks.

4.2 Types of management theory

We can make a start in removing some of the confusion by providing a classification of the broad types of managerial theory. It should be noted that the various types of theory are focused on answering very different problems or questions which are rarely connected or linked. Some examples of recent research are given in Table 4.1 to illustrate the types. Figure 4.1 shows the relative positions of such theories on an overall 'map' of management theory.

Type	Issues discussed	Examples	Comment
A Individual manager behaviour (How to behave as a manager)	**1. Great men biographies**	Sloan, Iacocca	Role models as prescriptions
	2. Empirical role studies	Carlson, Stewart, Sayles, Mintzberg, Burns, Lupton, Marples	Analysis of complexity of roles played
	3. Behavioural science prescriptions	McGregor, Blanchard, Herzberg	Theories about how to handle people in organizations
B Manager–subordinate relations (How to lead and integrate people in systems)	**4. Leadership**		Covers different aspects of leading and integrating
	– Traits	Bingham	
	– Philosophies	McGregor, Edström	
	– Styles	Likert, Blake, Bakke, Maccoby	
	– Power	Dalton, Cartwright	
	– Behaviour	Whyte, Walker, Sayles	
	– Work tasks	Carlson, Thurley-Wirdenius	
	– Contingent behaviour	Fiedler, Vroom-Yetton	

Table 4.1 *Types of management theory*

Type	Issues discussed	Examples	Comment
C Organizational/system design (Factors in planning systems)	5. Functions	Fayol, Drucker	Factors which make management different in different organizations
	6. National culture	England, Hofstede	
	7. Environmental uncertainty	Burns-Stalker, Woodward, Lawrence-Lorsch	
D Management processes (What management have to do)	8. Decision-making – Rational – Satisficing	Schumpeter, Mintzberg Simon, Cyert-March	Activities and processes required
	9. Techniques	Drucker, Kepner-Tregoe	
E Planning for change (How managers should plan and organize change programmes)	10. Strategic management	Ansoff	Critical aspects to watch in change situations
	11. Organizational culture/ development	Schein, Bennis	
	12. Change management	Tichy, Beckard, Argyris	

Table 4.1 *continued*

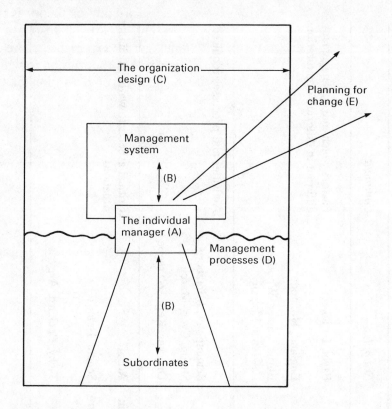

Figure 4.1 *Possible theoretical relations of types of management theory. (Based on Table 4.1)*

4.3 What is missing?

Figure 4.1 is based on an overview of the management literature. It should not be interpreted as meaning that management theory is, in reality, provided for managers in an integrated form. On the contrary, managers will normally point to the fact that academic or business school research is more and more concentrated on specialized technical issues which are studied as problems in their own right and are quite separate from (a) the type of context in which these problems have to be solved, and (b) the type of managerial action which is required within that context to solve the problem. In a word, the academic researchers have concentrated on studying and solving aspects of the managerial situation, *whereas it is the fact of the interdependence of these aspects within a system context which is so difficult for managers to deal with.*

This means that from the point of view of practicing managers, Fig. 4.1 should look more like Fig. 4.2. Each body of theory is not related to each other, and more important, is difficult to relate to management practice and actual managerial experience. This is partly because of the lack of distinction within theories as to which type of manager is being addressed and lack of definition of the level of the issue discussed.

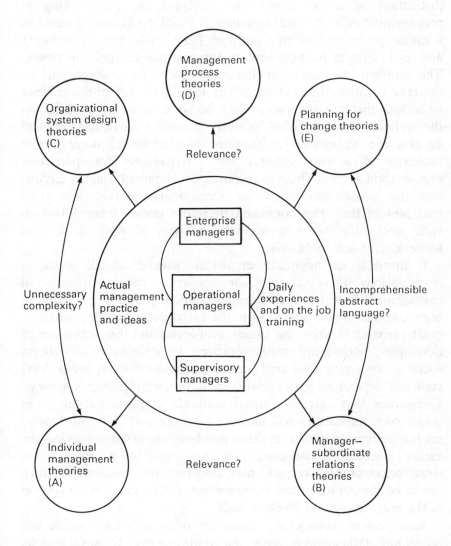

Figure 4.2 *Management theory as perceived by practicing managers.*

Management theory frequently does not cope adequately with the problem of reality for managers trying to separate out whether they are dealing with an individual or personal issue, a group issue and an organizational issue, *all at the same time*. At present there is a new tendency in management literature to reduce everything to issues which require an individual response.

As discussed in Chapter Three the concept of management itself is still confused. Harbison and Myers in 1959 made the useful distinction of three aspects of management: (a) looking at management as a technical resource, (b) looking at management as a status system or élite (the question here is *who* is management), and (c) looking at management as persons with authority or power. The problem has remained that many books on management do not take account of the effect of (b) and (c) on any of the policies or actions that are advocated. Such books frequently specialize on the techniques which could be used to solve a particular problem or else are attempted justifications of the use of management authority at a very general level. Arguments for particular organizational needs (human resource development, quality circles) and the consequent need for management action are good examples of this. The confusion therefore comes from a lack of clear distinction between accurate analysis of *what* exists and scenarios of *what could* exist.

If there is no adequate empirical research at all levels in organizations there is a clear tendency for discussions of management to reflect only top management perceptions. Even in organizations which are not particularly authoritarian, there is much research to show the isolation of levels and the difficulties of developing 'bottom-up' communications. Companies which rely on social surveys may find that accurate responses from lower level staff will depend on appropriate action following previous surveys. Companies that rely on formal methods of participation or of better communications will likewise discover that this will depend on the actions that may or may not have occurred following the earlier meetings. Those companies that argue the necessity for a clear 'organizational culture' may find that the 'culture' will turn out to be the values of top management, rather than an expression of the real views of all levels of staff.

Management theory still tends to offer solutions which are essentially static answers, assuming continuity over time. Of course, not everything changes all the time, but it could be argued that advanced societies are increasingly moving into areas of uncertainty and change, and traditional rules may not be appropriate. What is necessary is a framework which emphasizes possible changes at the same time as maintaining the viability of the system.

Management theory also rarely provides adequate models or explanations of essential changes taking place within organizations, for example in the increasingly polarized conflicts in Western Europe over 'rationalization' (the shutting down of inefficient plants, demanning exercises, simplification procedures, etc.). There needs to be an understanding of the objectives and patterns of thinking behaviour, both of the rationalizers and those resisting change, e.g. middle management. Research in the 1960s on site management behaviour in the construction industries in Sweden and the UK showed that many such managers relied on the 'programmes' (in Simon's sense) derived from their previous experience in order to solve current problems. For example, if a subcontractor had on a previous occasion taken a short-cut in completing an operation in order to save cost, it would be likely that site managers would tend to expect all subcontractors to behave in the same way. Very often in situations found in construction the constraints and beliefs of the parties concerned were fairly immutable, so the suspicions of site management might well be justified.

In a word, traditional management consists of ideas and recipes, culled from experience arrived at in a random and *ad hoc* manner. (This is shown within the circle at the centre of Fig. 4.2). Such managers may be very effective within the closed systems of traditional industry, but not surprisingly resist changes with considerable bitterness.

The rationalizers, on the other hand, tend to come from business schools and institutions of higher education and try to apply their analytical training to arrive at abstract formulations of new policies. Such training in business schools has often been a highly competitive experience and the schools tend to emphasize the use of economic and quantitative criteria for performance measurement, even in the areas of so called human resource management. Such a training does not lead to sympathy with traditional management. It is often very difficult for these two groups to understand each other (see Graves' port authority study, 1986).

Education and training in management theories, because of the tendency to emphasize principles, techniques, frameworks and prescriptions, appears to encourage the planning of change by specialist groups based on such abstract knowledge. A good example is that of corporate planning teams, who may be well versed in the theoretical problems of the management of change, but who reject or are disinterested in potential alternative solutions which may be developed from the ideas of other organization members, especially those from a traditional background. This leads to suboptimal solutions being enforced on unwilling or unenthusiastic lower level staff.

Although there may be many books on management as a subject, the reality is that ideas on management are highly fragmented. Management as a term is confounded between different levels, functions and occupational specializations. In actual organizations all occupational and professional groups have developed some ideas on authority (and power) in their training and these ideas become merged into the concepts and policies followed by particular organizations.

Although formal management theory may therefore mainly reflect the ideas of consultants and business school teachers, it does need to be stressed that the actual 'knowledge in use' theories believed in by practising managers need also to be explored and understood. The gap between these two is a fundamental problem preventing improvement of management performance.

5 The management of change

5.1 The basis for a European approach

The best starting point for designing a new European approach is to take the scepticism of local practising managers about academic managerial theory very seriously indeed. There is very little sense in adding to academic research in this field, if new ideas and propositions cannot be tested by actual practice. Management theory is worth little as an academic study on its own; essentially this is a body of knowledge leading to policy prescriptions. These have then to be tested as to their validity in many different situations. *The key is to provide a framework and approach which will allow and encourage practising managers at all levels to take new initiatives.* Such initiatives need also to be evaluated by collaboration between managers and other organizational actors, with the help of 'third party' researchers and consultants. In this way the 'gap' between theory and 'knowledge in use' can be eliminated.

The only alternative to this approach is to rely on the journalists' and consultants' accounts of managerial wisdom – as demonstrated above in numerous books of leading businessmen and of management gurus. This is bound to be highly simplistic and ideological in nature. We have already noted the political implications of this trend. It is not difficult to forecast the conflicts that are likely to arise in Europe from top management actions based on copying the decisions of supposedly 'excellent' American companies or successful Japanese firms and entrepreneurs.

The approach advocated here assumes that three elements have to be fused together:

(*a*) the practical 'knowledge in use' of managers who are experienced in their roles;

(b) social science research on the nature of organizational behaviour in work systems in different societies;

(c) experiential knowledge (judgement) on the process and direction of strategic changes which are possible and necessary (given the current state of the world economy and of the social and political situation).

The philosophical and value assumptions made here are that:

(a) it is desirable to be able to allow rational choices to be made with the maximum discussion possible, given constraints arising from the urgency of many of the changes required;

(b) the precise changes needed within each enterprise will be different;

(c) these changes should be decided by those who know the situation best;

(d) it is possible and useful to provide a framework to allow new thinking about change to take place;

(e) it is necessary to allow experimental changes to be evaluated and compared between organizations.

Although such a careful approach may appear to be somewhat unexciting and lacking drama, this is not necessarily so. As the pressures for internationalization increase – 1992 is now on the agenda of many boards of directors in Europe – so does the pace and scale of changes required increase. This gives strategic direction for the management of change.

5.2 A framework for considering the management of change

Objectives for change

Objectives can be ranked in a hierarchy. Precise goals and objectives have to be decided relative to a specific situation and its expected development. If that situation is highly turbulent then limited goals may have to be accepted on the grounds that it is probable that in the long run all plans have to be modified. Such limited objectives may be seen as supporting more long-term goals, however, which may only be reached after a long period of pursuing intermediate goals.

In any system the various parties represented (e.g. workers, unions, supervisors, staff, top management, external bodies) are likely to perceive different possibilities for change and to have very different priorities about the need for change in different areas. The extent of possible consensus on changes will vary widely.

Agreement on the objectives for change cannot be assumed but must be created. This agreement can be achieved by different strategies (discussed below), but it is likely that some process of negotiation will always be necessary. This becomes easier if a number of objectives are attempted simultaneously, so that, for example, improved production could be combined with attempts to improve the work environment and individual satisfaction.

Motivation for change

The planning of change by an external expert acting on his own – no matter how relevant – is unlikely to achieve significant results even if formally accepted. Motivation for change has two essential conditions:

(a) Some type of imaginative scenario for the future must be defined, discussed and understood.

(b) The changes proposed must include some changes which are seen as of the greatest salience to the parties concerned.

There is therefore little alternative to the involvement of all levels of managers and others affected in the discussion of possible changes step by step. Some degree of 'ownership' of the change programme and its objectives by managers and others is also essential.

Strategies for changes

In the literature on change strategies four types can be distinguished:

(a) Those based on power, either exercised unilaterally, e.g. top-down management, or bilaterally as in union – management negotiations. (This strategy will be called Type I.)

(b) Those based on a formal method or programme of change, such as a systematic recruitment scheme or a packaged training programme. (This strategy will be called Type II.)

(c) Those based on a new factual investigation or analysis of the situation. (This strategy will be called Type III.)

(d) Those based on the use of problem – solving groups among those steering the system or being steered by the system. (This strategy will be called Type IV.)

Such strategies have been argued as alternatives according to the values and the philosophy of the writer. In reality, simple strategies based on one approach are most unlikely to achieve results. Combinations are always necessary, and the essential design problem is the question of deciding the initial strategy, and how and when the alternative strategies can be brought in to support and quicken the pace of change. It follows that the involvement of all parties in the design of strategies as they emerge is also essential.

Each change strategy has to deal with a set of problems in a particular sequence, viz.:

(*a*) What should be the objectives for the change strategy?

(*b*) What is going to be the 'motor of change' that will carry through the changes? What is the broad method or form of intervention planned?

(*c*) What new information, ideas, insights, arguments are necessary in order to convince people of the logical necessity of making such changes?

(*d*) How far have others accepted the need for actively pursuing the solution of problems, suggesting innovations and offering positive comments and suggestions on previous managerial actions?

If the change strategy takes (a) as the starting point as the main problem and, for example, the managing director of a firm decides on his own judgement that the firm has to go in a new direction, then this can be classified as a *power-based strategy* (Type I), at least in its initial stage. If the management decides that the real problem is to design an effective change programme (b) and calls on the services of an expert for this purpose, then this is known as a *method-based strategy* (Type II). If the major initial problem is seen as lack of information or data and an expert is hired to produce a report on the subject (c) then this can be called an *empirical/rational strategy* (Type III). Lastly, if the first decision is the need to get active problem-solving groups going in the organization (for example, quality circles) in order to motivate staff, then the strategy is called here a *problem solution strategy* (Type IV).

Combinations of strategies are normal; what is important is the type of combination and type of sequence followed. Some examples may make this clear.

(a) An agreement between management and labour unions to develop greater job flexibility (I) would probably develop into a systematic programme of work restructuring (II), possibly followed by the setting up of problem-solving groups to help the training on the job of those doing new jobs (IV). This strategy could be formally described therefore as follows:

Objective setting → Work restructuring → Problem-solving groups

or

I→II→IV

(b) The hiring of consultants by a board on their possible product development policy would be followed by a report (III) and then a decision of the board on new products (I) and then a R&D programme (II) followed by evaluation by a sales/marketing group (IV). This could be described as follows:

III→I→II→IV.

Strategies therefore involve sequences which can be seen as cycles of activity. Some strategies involve slowly moving from stage to stage; others involve a quick set of cycles of activities, involving different levels of employees. It is possible to describe strategies in terms of the very 'long wave' approaches adopted by managers over a period of years; in this case the small and limited interventions which take place during this time may conflict with the overall approach, but only up to a certain point. A programme of employee participation will be destroyed by too many arbitrary non-participative decisions taken by top management.

The evaluation of the change programme

Successful change has to be perceived as relevant to the actual needs of each of the parties to the change and also must be credible in that the results of the change are accepted as valid. Evaluation is therefore an essential part of the process. Evaluation, however, does not mean a simple before and after measure, which is impossible if the strategy is complex and multi-stage. Relevant criteria for judging the results achieved need to be agreed stage by stage. The actual data also have to be collected stage by stage, as well as during the process itself.

It follows that considerable thought has to be given to deciding the type of information which will yield the best indication of any results achieved. Such information will always be selective and will never be one hundred per cent conclusive.

It should always be possible to find some information to test the actual result achieved, but this process also depends on real collaboration among the parties and their interest in testing how far the programme has been successful.

For research purposes the internal process of evaluation described above needs to be supplemented by an external 'meta-evaluation', in which different change programmes can be compared systematically in terms of contrasting strategies, different situations and results. In the internal evaluation the Hawthorne-effect is a positive supportive factor. In the meta-evaluation it needs to be controlled.

The third-party role and management

Originally the planning of change involved the role of an external consultant or action researcher who was the expert, who tried to analyse the situation, design changes, carry them out and evaluate their success. It is increasingly difficult to find situations where such an expert role is acceptable. In addition to that it is doubtful if one person can combine such a range of expertise. Too often the external expert is steered by the situation to prove that his intervention was correct. Third-party roles, however, are likely to be necessary at every stage of the process of change, i.e. in diagnosis, helping to achieve the setting of objectives, suggesting a design, running the programme, helping with evaluation. In most situations third-party roles should therefore be shared among different staff specialists both internal to the organization and coming from external bodies.

It is likely that external third-party roles will be advisers to senior enterprise management, but it is certainly possible that change can be initiated by operational or supervisory management and that these may call on the services of an 'expert'.

It should be noted that strategies II and III are the most likely to depend on the role of a third party.

Such an approach goes far beyond the current debate on the importance of defining 'business strategy'. This is conventionally taught as an analysis of choices for top management, particularly related to choosing their product portfolio and location of operations (Ansoff, 1984). The approach here combines such strategic choice thinking with an emphasis on the issues of changing the structure and processes of the actual organization. This involves – as stated – utilizing the 'knowledge in use' of managers and employees within a particular set of subcultures, but also of developing the capacity for strategic judgement on the part of decision-makers and their skills for carrying it out. All of these aspects are important. If any are missing, failure will result.

6 Enterprise management: strategic choice in transforming organizations

6.1 Different forms of enterprise management

Conventionally, writers such as Chandler (1962) and Williamson (1977) have distinguished the corporate structure of large firms by contrasting functionally integrated single structures (U form firms) from those organized into product or geographical divisions which then operate on a semi-autonomous basis (M form firms). It is argued by Williamson that the latter will operate at a higher level of profitability compared to corresponding size firms based on the U form. The distinction between the M form and the device of a holding company (the H form) is clearly a matter of degree and scope of internal company control systems and the amount of 'steering' displayed by the headquarters. Much of the debate about the relative proportion and profitability of these types of structures (Chandler, 1962) is dubious, given the lack of published information on the actual control processes used by firms.

For our purposes here it is important clearly to point out the problems of defining 'enterprise management'. Our definition above (Chapter Three) assumes that all levels of the management hierarchy above that of supervisory management will be members of enterprise management in U form firms, but that 'operational management' can be deemed to exist if there is an attempt to account for subunits of the firm in terms of a business unit, i.e. in both M forms and H forms of the enterprise. In extreme forms of the H form, there is so little at the holding company level that the enterprise would have to be defined at the subsidiary company level. These are questions of degree, not of black and white, and the meaning of enterprise will have to be decided case by case.

In each enterprise we will find one or two levels of board and a hierarchy of managers under the chief executive, probably organized in functional departments. We have called this a 'social system', which implies that there is a degree of interdependence in the roles and activities of managers and departments. Decisions, taken formally at board level or by lower levels of enterprise management, are deemed to be the basis of 'policy' which is imposed downwards throughout the enterprise. The junior ranks of enterprise management will be either specialists, support staff or staff charged with communications with operating managers.

6.2 Strategic choice

The functions of 'enterprise management' are:

(*a*) to maintain the running of the whole enterprise on a viable basis by the handling of routine disturbances;

(*b*) to introduce innovations to avoid perceived future problems or disturbances;

(*c*) to introduce changes of direction and goals, new programmes, procedures and modifications to the structure of the enterprise. This implies that managerial decisions have to balance the maintenance of the whole system against programmes designed to change it.

The argument here is that the threat to European competitiveness is such and the degree of economic restructuring needed is so great that the management of change, i.e. (*b*) and (*c*), has to be given priority. Although the precise nature of those change goals has to be determined locally, it can be argued strongly that many European enterprises need to design and pursue radically different business strategies in terms of product development and improvements of existing product lines. Such business strategies almost certainly require major shifts in the structure, processes and methods used by enterprise management. This in turn has consequences at the individual level. Managers have to change jobs, be retrained, learn to work with new colleagues in new ways and learn new styles of leadership. All this requires the definition of an overall strategy of change to give direction and purpose to the more detailed interventions that are needed issue by issue.

We can summarize the nature of strategic choice, therefore, as developing an overall approach which will, in a particular enterprise, meet one of the following goals:

(*a*) running, maintaining, consolidating the existing system;

(*b*) continually developing the existing system;

(*c*) radically changing (regenerating) the existing system into a new system;

(*d*) designing a new system (and sometimes also liquidating an old system).

Figure 6.1 demonstrates the nature of strategic choice and its implications for the three levels of management.

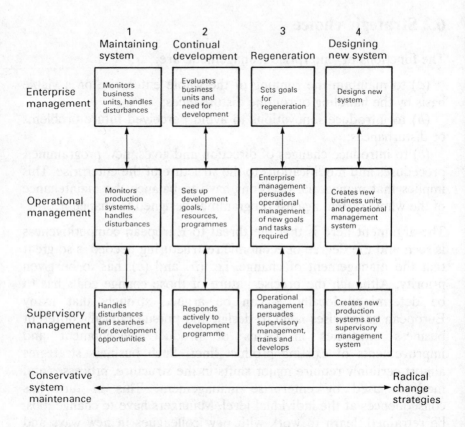

Figure 6.1 *Strategic choice and implications for levels and types of management.*

Innovation can start at any level, i.e. enterprises may try to innovate only at the supervisory management and/or operational management levels. The consequences will have implications for the rest of the organization. The decision on the level of change is therefore a very critical one.

In any actual case, an enterprise may have to move from (d) to (a) over time and then back at least to (c).

6.3 Designing a strategy

Research seems to indicate that the following problems have to be solved by enterprise management if they wish to have an appropriate strategy of change.

(a) *Searching*. This involves market research and internal studies, and concentrates on customer and employee needs, future social trends, etc.

(b) *Broadening vision and creating a style*. Enterprise management has to decide on new goals and ways of achieving those goals which are going to create identity.

(c) *Deepening the involvement of all levels of employees*. It is necessary to obtain the active support of all levels of staff for the new direction.

(d) *Setting new standards of performance and developing new products*. New standards and new products are both necessary and have to be determined by careful study and agreement.

(e) *Initiating (selective) action to change roles/people/structures and develop human potential (knowledge/skills/attitudes)*. Change programmes will need to be rooted in much higher human performance.

(f) *Evaluating/discussing/reviewing problems and mistakes*. A critical review of decisions taken by the enterprise management team responsible for the change programme should be encouraged.

This model of the strategic change process can be described in terms of the frame of reference in Chapter Five. The first three problems (stages (a)–(c)) can be seen as related to a typical empirical/rational (Type III) strategy. The action stage of standard setting, etc. planned through a participative process of staff involvement group ((c)–(d)) could be classified as a method-based (Type II) strategy. Actual initiatives to change organization structures, transfer staff, arrange training, etc. ((d)–(e)) may not be easy to carry out on a consensual basis as too many managers may see themselves as losing out in the process. This problem may well require a tough power-based decision (Type I) as it could involve very unpopular decisions. Lastly, the evaluation stage should essentially be carried out both by external and internal groups. The former requires an independent expert assessment (Type III strategy) but the latter would involve setting up a set of problem-solving groups to review the strategy (Type IV).

Altogether, therefore, this approach is rather complex but very comprehensive (see Fig. 6.2). As a cycle, the overall strategy required can be described as in Fig. 6.3.

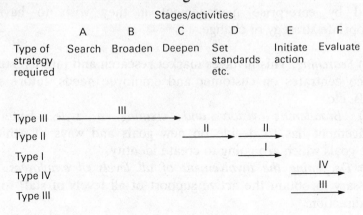

Figure 6.2 *Stages of overall strategy required by enterprise management.*

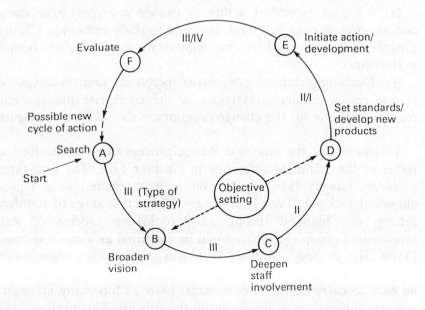

Figure 6.3 *Enterprise strategy for innovation shown as a cycle of activities.*

6.4 Testing the model

This framework can now be tested on a recent construction company case ('The Diös case', Lundin and Wirdenius, 1989).

A: Search

The motivation for attempting any radical change in an organization arises from an emerging crisis which is perceived by some or most of the actors concerned, usually top management. A certain degree of threat is therefore necessary before action will be taken. Search procedures are necessary to define the threat and possible remedial action.

The Diös case

The company in this case was a medium sized construction company in Sweden, part of a larger concern. It employed 200 permanent staff and 800 workers in 1984. The main product was house (apartment block) building.

In 1984 there was a big financial loss, which followed years of high profitability. Although this took place in a period of retrenchment for the construction industry, the chief executive was not satisfied with the idea that the loss was simply part of the market deterioration. He believed that this was a real crisis for the company and required radical change. This crisis was probably not perceived by the staff in general.

After discussion with the top management of the overall concern he came to the following conclusions:

(a) That the fierce competition had made them sign building contracts at far too low prices.

(b) That they had got behind in the technological development process.

(c) That there were internal relations and motivation problems, among other things owing to low personnel turnover and long tenure of key people.

He decided to survey client perceptions of contractor services by hiring a consultant to carry out a PDS study (problem detection survey). The conclusions pointed to the need for better customer service.

Comment

The case is a very typical one. The search procedure was only directed externally at clients, in this case because the CEO had been in the company for more than 20 years and was very close to contract operations, so he felt that he understood the internal situation. The search procedure may take place generally to provide data for new understanding or it can be used to provide data to support judgements that have already been arrived at. In latter cases it is frequently necessary to involve a third party to allow independent gathering of information.

B: Broaden vision

Strategy design involves diagnosis of organizational and external conditions, knowledge of alternative scenarios of change, predictions of likely effects, beliefs about critical objectives. This is therefore a very complex process. The creation of understanding and excitement about future change requires a 'broad brush' vision of alternative possibilities, typically contrasting the 'old' with the 'new'. Successful innovation therefore requires the translation of a complex diagnosis into a simple vision. This is often seen as the essence of leadership.

The Diös case

The basic vision of the CEO was to shift the orientation of the company from a production-based to a customer-based framework. The diagnosis was focused on the need to avoid loss-making tenders for public and private building (due to local competition) and to concentrate on continuity of service, i.e. insuring that clients were pleased with the contract work quality and therefore wished to continue with new contracts. This had therefore to be translated into a drive within the company for much higher standards of performance and service.

The CEO started by gathering the whole permanently employed staff of 200 people to an orientation meeting in order to create awareness of the crisis and commitment to the renewal project. He had engaged two external management consultants as inspirers and performers of the 'rough work' called for in the realization of the project.

At this meeting he described the economic development of the company up till today's situation characterized by a big loss. He put up successively increasing profitability targets for the next three years. The aim of the project was stated as being:

(a) to get better profitability;
(b) to get better co-ordination;

(c) to get more satisfied customers;
(d) to get more satisfaction on the job;
(e) to have work also tomorrow.

Eighteen working groups were formed to be led by department and project managers chosen by the CEO. Group work was to be run in three stages according to a time schedule settled beforehand: producing ideas and suggestions, evaluating suggestions and implementing chosen solutions.

Comment

It is interesting to note that the crucial meeting of all staff in the company had five objectives:

(a) to create awareness among staff of the crisis;
(b) to give a new vision for company operations;
(c) to set down targets for performance for several years;
(d) to set up working groups for detailed involvement of all permanent staff;
(e) to impose a timetable and the main structure for involvement discussions. (Each group had freedom within this structure.)

In essence this was therefore a Type I power-centred intervention, but it quickly led to problem-solving (Type IV) actions. To place so many objectives into one meeting was clearly a risky strategy which actually succeeded.

C: Deepen involvement of staff

There are three aspects of participation in decision-making: the process of involvement seen as an educational process for participants; the use of the opportunity for negotiation on behalf of interest groups (to change the agenda and objectives of the change initiative); the use of participation to allow expertise to be contributed to effective problem solution.

The Diös case

The groups were assigned different problem areas, related to the three main stages of a construction project: 'tender', 'during construction' and 'after construction'. The starting point for group work was the previous survey of customer opinions on company operations and the performance of the construction industry as a whole.

The groups were left to decide how to carry out their work. They were supposed to deliver a report to the CEO and the consultants every week. At the second stage all suggestions to solve company problems were listed (142 in number). After that a joint evaluation was made of solutions: how useful and worth concentrating on they were, in view of economy, available time and other resources (22 remaining). This evaluation work was carried out partly in the individual groups, partly in joint one-day meetings with group leaders, consultants and the CEO. A central group led by the CEO dealt with general questions, e.g. the position of the company in relation to competitors, relations to clients, the strong and weak points of the organization.

Comment

It is clear that the role of the CEO in stimulating, planning and motivating the participation process was a very strong one. The group activities varied in effectiveness but there is evidence that all three aspects of participation were included. Although the problem solution objective was dominant, the groups came out with a set of policy objectives which was not designed by the CEO. To some extent, the interests of particular interest groups, e.g. site agents, were expressed through the group process, i.e. negotiation did take place. Certainly in many, but not all, cases participation led to a greater understanding of the company needs. The strategy included both a Type I and Type IV approach carefully balanced.

D: Set standards/develop new products

Stating a vision is never sufficient; setting standards and deciding on new products or targets are lower level objectives following from the overall vision. Sometimes such objectives will include entirely new activities. Such specification of objectives needs to follow detailed technical discussion if it is to be appropriate and realizable.

The Diös case

At the third stage the real reorganization of the company was made, implying a transformation of production groups into business groups (with local responsibility for client relations and economic results) and implementation of preferred solutions. Actions and initiatives aimed at the following six main areas:

'To do the right things'

(a) *Tender.* Calculating and designing tenders to meet client demands.

(b) *Maintenance.* Developing the unexploited area of building maintenance.

(c) *Business groups.* Making every production group member responsible for profitability.

'To do things right'

(d) *The 3% project.* Saving 3% of turnover – 700 million Swedish crowns.

(e) *Guarantee work.* Developing guarantee work in order to enhance client good will and prevent future problems.

(f) *Training and development.* Setting up individual training schemes and making every one responsible for getting needed training, stimulating general development initiatives.

After six months the CEO once again summoned all staff to a meeting in which he informed about the current state of the renewal project the reorganization had decided upon and the coming development effort in the six areas. He also reminded the audience of the aim to increase profitability by steps over three years. As a confirmation each employee received a pamphlet entitled *'Six ways for us in the company to do better business'*, which briefly described initiatives that needed to be taken jointly in the above-mentioned six areas in order to achieve a renewal of the company and increased profitability.

Comment

This case at this stage seems a classic example of an effective process for setting standards and deciding on new areas of activity. The six areas in the pamphlet were highly stimulating for most staff and concentrated attention on crucial priorities. The actual strategy was, however, more complex than it appeared to be. The method was suggested by the consultants and therefore could be seen as a Type II approach. On the other hand, the direction was closely steered by the CEO and this had an element of power direction (Type I). It also, however, reflected genuine discussion in the groups and therefore was partially a Type IV approach.

E: Initiate action to change

Having gone through such a complex process for deciding objectives and the approach, the model in Fig. 6.2, assures that actual changes are then implemented in a planned and systematic manner (Type II approach).

The Diös case

From the 1st of December 1985, the CEO formally announced the implementation of a new company organization based on independent business groups. Local managers were all involved in project groups within the business groups. Some staff had to change their roles and greater flexibility was introduced in local staff groups.

Later the CEO brought together the staff of each department to discuss the current distribution of responsibility. He then also informed the staff about his proposed follow-up of each construction project, through checklists to be filled out by project managers in collaboration with site agents. Furthermore, he made follow-up visits to construction sites and arranged meetings with site management.

Initiatives were taken to start a new business activity (maintenance) in collaboration with a recently founded subsidiary company. A central development council was also founded with instructions to distribute the considerable funds set aside for development purposes in the company.

About six months after the last general meeting the CEO sent out written information to all staff on the state of the six development areas and on business progress, showing that the profitability curve had turned and the company was on the right track.

After another half year the CEO again summoned all staff for a detailed information session on the state of the project, on business prospects and on future plans. He stated that he was impressed by what had been accomplished in two years, even though there was a part still left to handle. It was now time to start the 'guarantee work of rebuilding' to extend over the next three quarters. After that the project could be terminated and the staff get together for a celebration party. He pointed at the areas that should be particularly considered during the termination period in order to reach the profitability target (increase the share of company-sponsored projects and bargaining contracts, develop the maintenance sector, make materials handling more effective, and intensify personnel development and training). The meeting was closed with applause by participants.

The termination party was held in May 1987 after a reorganization of the concern, carried out at the turn of the year and implying fusion of the three central construction companies and sale of the other two.

Comment

This case shows that implementation is not necessarily a smooth programmed (Method II) type activity. On the contrary, the CEO demonstrated an enormous energy in visibly talking with all staff, both local, regional and project staff. He got reports continuously on the process and then reacted to that information. This is therefore a highly directed Type IV problem solution operation which was on the whole very well received by the staff. The interventions were seen as realistic and the CEO had great credibility due to his knowledge of events and of local 'culture'.

F: Evaluate

Evaluation can focus on short-term changes or on major system change. It can be a short cycle feedback process or a more systematic longer term data collection by third parties. Both are necessary in such a planned strategy of change. System change, however, is difficult to prove. Innovators can easily claim success and cynics can quote failures. The degree of consensus over the criteria used is itself important for judging 'success'.

The Diös case

Data on reactions and effects were gathered by researchers at interviews every six months with a representative sample (about 20%) of the permanent staff, including the CEO. Moreover, observational data were collected at information meetings, at gatherings of group leaders in the renewal project, at follow-up visits to construction sites by the CEO, at top management meetings, and when feeding researcher observations back to management and other staff.

Views expressed by management and other staff at interviews are summarized below.

Views on company situation

Many respondents expressed their appreciation of the resolute acting of the CEO by summoning a general meeting and in that way evoking awareness of a crisis among the staff group. An information meeting held by the new corporate CEO obviously helped to spread understanding of the profitability crisis. The degree of awareness differed between departments, who themselves had varying levels of profitability.

The polarization between office staff and supervisors on construction sites was seen as a problem related to increased central control and the perception that there was less attention being paid by management to improving technology and achieving production targets.

People also felt concern for the notion that the construction business might be sold or discontinued by owners (this was a family-owned firm).

Views on group work

With few exceptions, statements made on group work activities expressed approval of its design (the use of vertical and horizontally mixed groups). The need for greater contact and exchange of ideas across groups in order to tear down barriers and create new ways of thinking was stressed. General participation was considered useful as every one was stimulated to give views and suggestions. It was also seen to be important in an unfamiliar change situation that some (visible) action was taking place.

A few respondents, however, found that the discussions to a great extent dealt with old and well-known suggestions, ideas they had not yet managed to put into action. The view was also expressed that the group work took much time and was extremely hard work. In some cases motivation was low and follow-up information was lacking.

Views on the organization change

Several respondents expressed their appreciation of the CEO's efforts. Those who were interviewed during the first months after the reorganization looked at the change with some concern or even scepticism, particularly in view of difficulties in consequence of replacements, enlarged tasks and internal cost allocation. Others, having been interviewed later, generally viewed changes in a more positive and optimistic way, such changes implying greater autonomy and local control.

The statements show that the organizational change itself was the element of the renewal project which created the greatest feelings of insecurity and anxiety at the prospect of the future. Some staff had wished for a quicker decision to be taken; others wanted consultant support in carrying through the change.

Views on the renewal project as a whole

The majority of the respondents viewed the future with confidence and thought that the renewal project had been of use by creating increased awareness of profitability targets and of the six development areas given priority (tender, maintenance, business groups, save 3% of turnover, guarantee work and development/training). They also mentioned effects such as better planning, quality improvements, better internal and external co-operation, and a stronger company identity, effects seen as having influenced profitability indirectly. The statements also showed that they appreciated the CEO's personal efforts in the project.

Many of the respondents found it difficult to get time both for ordinary work and project activities. They therefore suggested that the project should have been carried on more quickly and information also should have been given to various external parties to forestall them from constantly asking questions. Their wish for widened co-operation from site agents and supervisors obviously springs from the alienation felt by field staff from the office activities. It could easily happen that field staff feel excluded from such a project and that production viewpoints are not considered sufficiently. This can be a reason for such staff to regard the new suggestions as unoriginal, difficult to use, theoretical or perhaps as being applied already.

The strong paternalistic organizational culture and the attitudes of the long-tenured staff were both seen as a barrier against reorientation of the construction firm. Alarm was expressed at the project by some, considering what a new management team and a younger owner might do with the company.

Comment

In this case, the economic success of the project could be partially explained by the change in market situation. On the other hand, the growth of the market went together with the changes. The major issue arising from the evaluation is the complexity of combining innovation and ordinary work roles at the same time. The skills required were often very different. In spite of the difficulties of changing the construction situation, however, there does seem to be evidence of a large amount of consensus among the staff on the nature of the changes which had to be carried out and the relative success of the project.

Conclusions

The model in Fig. 6.2, therefore, can be seen as useful for analysing the Diös case, although it is obvious that the detailed stages may vary somewhat in the strategy used according to the context. The logic of the model, however, can be seen as a prototype for a European approach to the management of change for enterprise management.

7 Taking production seriously

7.1 The social context of 'production systems' in Europe

It has been argued above that the key to understanding so much of the special character of the work situation, the work ethic and work relationships in European countries lies with the long and slow history of industrialization from the late medieval period onwards. European domination of the world in the nineteenth century depended on the factory system developed from skilled craft (guild) labour, the use of semi-skilled female operatives and the existence of specialist *Meister* or *contremaître* (craft foremen). It also depended on the skills and knowledge of technical specialists – engineers – who were usually trained in specialist vocational schools and through on-the-job tuition as apprentices. There is no doubt that such specialists had considerable prestige and authority in countries such as France, Germany and Sweden and this lent considerable status to working in organizations using advanced technology. Even though countries such as Great Britain did not have this *Technik* tradition, it is still true that a career in a large engineering firm had considerable prestige in the decades up to the First World War.

The survival of aristocratic values in the upper and ruling classes is usually given as a reason for the neglect of technology in the case of the United Kingdom (Wiener, 1981). A second factor is the importance of the financial and commercial centres, particularly the City of London, which meant that white-collar careers were highly successful. Whatever the reason, however, there is no doubt that by the 1970s there was a clear trend for university graduates to avoid jobs in manufacturing industry. The slump of the early 1980s accelerated this trend. The rationale was accepted that the United States showed that advanced economies were largely service sector economies and that automation would quickly eliminate a large number of jobs in manufacturing. Even countries where engineering and factory management has attracted many élite graduates, such as Sweden or Germany, started to notice that 'production' no longer had the appeal of the past. Working in small firms in the service industry or as independent consultants began to have much greater attraction. Salaries in manufacturing have reflected this trend over the last ten to fifteen years. The dramatic rise of salary levels in the City of London 'Big Bang' revolution is only an extension of this trend.

This shift in the relative status and importance of manufacturing *vis à vis* services is certainly one factor mitigating against graduates from higher education wanting to be involved with the management of production systems. Another factor was the existence of traditional promotion routes from the shop floor to supervisory management. If university students or graduates were found getting shop-floor experience as workers or foremen, it would not be for long. The core of supervisory management were promotees from worker positions and they could go no further. This system could be said to be at the root of the intense conservatism of shop-floor supervisors. What they knew had been learnt entirely within one local production system and often by observation and trial and error. Such 'knowledge in use' could be contrasted with theoretical knowledge learnt from libraries, books, laboratories and lectures. Those with academic knowledge were conveniently recruited into specialist functional jobs or through trainee schemes were brought into higher management by entry above the supervisory management level.

We have argued that the term 'production system' should be used as a general concept to cover all types of work systems which have a technological base and a definable set of inputs and outputs to the system. The term therefore is used here to refer to retail, transport, distribution, financial and insurance systems, etc., as well as manufacturing *per se*. As the technological base of the 'service' sector systems increases, however, so does it become clear that such systems begin to look like manufacturing and have the same effects. The 'grey-collar' worker in a uniform may be on shifts and under the type of strict controls and discipline which makes him or her indistinguishable from blue-collar or manual workers. Even young graduates on high salaries in the dealing rooms of the City of London are working very long hours and under considerable pressures in a particular type of 'production system'.

To summarize the argument, the 'post-industrial revolution' of service management, customer orientation, 'knowledge organizations' and information technology indeed succeeds in giving much of manufacturing industry the look of the past. High technology and scientific research based industry such as bio-technology are of course exceptions to this, for the moment at least. To work supervizing a production system means a role that involves detailed knowledge of the workings of the local technology and the habits, customs and ways of thinking and behaving of those employees running the system. There is a clear danger that such work is not attractive to graduates from higher education. The implication is that such social factors combine to ensure that supervisory management in the manufacturing sector is restricted to those promoted from the shop floor. Even in other types of production system, such as in transportation and services, the supervisory positions are of comparatively low status. This in turn can create a highly conservative climate among supervisors and may lead to considerable resistance to change.

7.2 The functions of supervisory management

Supervisory management is concerned with the steering and the effectiveness of production systems, that is it tries to deal with disturbances to the planned working and output of the system. This can be done by dealing with each contingency as it comes – crisis management – or by trying to predict what will happen and then taking steps to prevent it. There are likely to be disturbances which have occurred previously, for example machine breakdowns, but other problems may be encountered for the first time, such as the quality standards of new components. This can be shown diagramatically as in Fig. 7.1.

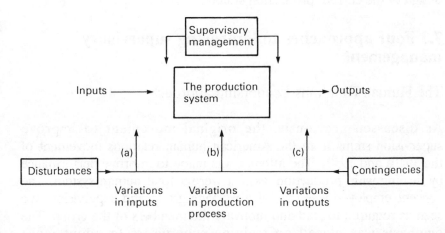

Figure 7.1 *Supervisory management seen as a function concerned with the steering and effectiveness of a production system.*

It follows that supervisory management is concerned with three types of performance standard:

(a) Specifying exactly the inputs required for a given production system performance level and meeting these specifications (*input efficiency*). These may be very difficult to achieve if the production system is exposed to large unexpected variations of supply (for example, for component supplies in assembly operations).

(b) Specifying the capacity for effective operation of the production system (*system efficiency*). This involves knowledge of the interrelationship between the various operations within the system and how this varies under different levels of output requirements. Measures of labour or capital productivity are too simple by themselves here. Supervisory management need to operate with a mental model of the whole system working effectively and to use this to diagnose deviations and the malfunctioning of the system. In service organizations, this requires knowledge of how each person is performing, e.g. the head waiter in a restaurant constantly monitors customer service. In complex technologies, the data may be fed to a single control room, e.g. in electricity supply.

(c) Specifying standards of output required by clients, customers or the next department in sequence in a manufacturing organization (*output efficiency*). This involves knowledge of service or product specifications and how these are varying according to demand. Supervisory management may be faced with large shifts in demand which cannot be met in the short run, but they always need to know what is possible and what is impossible, given the constraints of the design of the current production system.

7.3 Four approaches to improving supervisory management

The Human Relations Leadership approach

As discussed previously, the original movement to improve supervision stems from the American human relations movement of the 1940s and 1950s. The attempt was made to improve performance by dealing with 'production' as if it were a total human system. The concept employed was that of a working group and supervision was seen as required to lead and motivate the members of the group. The emphasis was placed on training supervisors to adopt more democratic and participative styles of supervision in order to support and motivate work groups to achieve norms. The problem here was that supervisors were rarely in a position to control the various types of disturbances affecting the system, and secondly that workers in many organizations saw little reason to change their established practices and norms to follow supervisors who were perceived as 'men in the middle' and not fully supported and respected by senior management or staff departments.

The Socio-Technical Redesign approach

This movement was not primarily concerned with production supervision effectiveness but mainly with improving QWL indicators for employees by redesigning the system. It became important in Western Europe in the 1960s and 1970s. Satisfaction, it was argued, would improve by such changes as the formation of semi-autonomous groups, capable of a whole range of skills and responsible for a 'whole' task. Supervisory management would then be mainly exercised by the group itself, so 'supervision' could be eliminated or at least reduced in its 'control' function.

The problem with this analysis was again that it concentrated on the human factor and the need to redesign the 'technical system' to fit human requirements. Many experiments in Scandianavia, West Germany and in the USA showed that the approach could lead to more effective production systems, but there was considerable neglect of the importance of external disturbances to the running of the system (see e.g. Forslin, 1989). Very few experiments, for example, dealt with 'output efficiency' in terms of customer requirements and how these could be better met. The emphasis on participation of employees in working groups tended to be seen as an end in itself.

Organization development (OD)

This movement was at its height in Europe in the 1960s and 1970s. The main concept was the need to develop a more open culture among managers, supervisors and employees so that problems could be brought into the open and discussed. It was very important as a component of industrial relations change in certain firms, and a detailed case study is given here to show the approval and the difficulties encountered.

The ICI Alpha Works supervisory project (April 1972 - December 1975)

Background

In the period from the mid 1960s onwards a number of changes were taking place in the company which seriously affected the supervisory role. The following case study is taken from the above project report by Bob King with his kind permission.

(a) Chargehands (first-line supervisors) had all been promoted to 'staff grades' (white-collar status) and were renamed assistant foremen in 1961. The manual trade unions persisted in trying to organize and secure negotiating rights for assistant foremen. Many assistant foremen, however, resisted this approach. However, the company in 1966 agreed that those assistant foremen in the locality of the Alpha Works who had been manual union members when they were promoted, had to retain their membership. This policy was greatly resented by many assistant foremen.

(b) Foremen were organized in a separate association and had considerable rights of representation over foremen's interests in the complex of factories in the area of the Alpha plant. A strong recruiting drive among supervisors had taken place nationally in the late 1960s (by one major white-collar union). The foremen's association therefore agreed nationally with the company and the manual workers' union that assistant foremen could elect accredited representatives (shop stewards) provided they were members of the supervisory branch of the manual unions. In short, the foremen and assistant foremen were under great pressure between competing unions.

(c) From the late 1960s the company had carried through a major change with the unions in the status of manual workers under the weekly staff agreement (WSA). Briefly, in the return for an annual salary system, workers were involved in negotiations which increased their role responsibilities, e.g. process workers were asked to take on certain maintenance duties. The negotiations for this agreement in the Alpha Works agreement were long and hard. Several consequences arose which increased supervisory anxiety and frustration.

First, the negotiations created a strong group of manual shop stewards who became familiar with the senior management of each works. The foremen frequently felt bypassed by these negotiations and the stewards were clear competitors to the foremen in influencing the workforce. Secondly, certain supervisory responsibilities were handed over to senior process workers and in some cases the two-level supervisory system was changed to a single-tier system. At the same time, planning departments took over certain planning responsibilities from foremen.

(d) A further factor in the early 1970s for the Alpha Works division was a considerable recession in trade and a redundancy programme which included foremen was set up.

(e) At the central level of the company in the late 1960s a major organizational development exercise was launched, in which OD consultants were trained and appointed to many divisions. The personnel department at the Alpha Works and the divisional headquarters were strongly affected by these ideas, as were many plant managers.

The supervisory situation

The Alpha Works employs some 1,850 weekly staff personnel (manual workers) in the three large chemical plants. Supervisors were divided between process supervising and an electrical instrument section which served the production areas. The works forms part of a very large complex of chemical plants in a number of divisions of the company. The supervisors formed a local foremen's association with a committee for the whole site. Approximately two-thirds of the foremen belonged to this association.

By 1972 both management and foremen were well aware of the following problems:

(a) Supervisors now had few promotion chances compared with previous opportunities some ten years earlier.

(b) Major capital investment had produced new plants with reduced manning levels and greatly increased technical complexity.

(c) The combination of the industrial relations developments noted above had resulted in a perceived reduction of authority for all foremen.

(d) The new status of workers was seen by supervisors as a considerable reduction of their differentials in terms of status, security and fringe benefits.

(e) The appraisal of the quality and performance of supervisors by managers was not high. They were seen as negative in their attitudes and old-fashioned in their thinking, and managers were sometimes reluctant to involve foremen in joint consultation exercises.

The philosophy behind the change strategy

By 1971 at Alpha Works management had established an OD process for discussing and 'working through' the problems of the various interests and sections in the works. Union-management workshops were organized 'to make people more aware of themselves, to make them more aware of other people around them and perhaps to give them some idea of how other groups behave'.

This type of 'process' objective in 1972 was extended specifically to the supervisory question. The senior personnel officer suggested that a limited supervisory development programme could be supported by the main management committee. In particular, discussions were to be focused on the problems perceived by the supervisors and these should be discussed with managers individually and in groups.

Objectives and goals

In January 1973, the deputy works manager suggested that the supervisory development programme should:

(*a*) try to define and analyse the nature of the supervisory problems;

(*b*) try to suggest areas in which supervisors could be expected to exercise a positive influence. These were stated as follows:

(1) Technical/operational goals

(1.1) Planning and co-ordination
    i. Workload of shifts
    ii. Target-setting – quantity and quality and in relation to budget
    iii. Equipment usage
    iv. (Long term) – shut-downs of plant (for maintenance)

(1.2) Monitoring and control
    i. Efficiencies
    ii. Material usage
    iii. Equipment performance

(2) Man management

(2.1) Positive and practical goals
    i. Communication (up and down)
    ii. Consultation (on ways and means – usage of human resources)

   iii. Continuous performance appraisal
   iv. Administration (holidays, leave, overtime)
   v. Selection/training/promotion

(2.2) Negative and practical goals
     e.g. Discipline

(2.3) Behavioural goals
     i. Facilitation – interface handling
     ii. Leadership (getting the best out of their team
        in a given situation)
     iii. 'Culture' establishment (the legitimacy of satisfying
        peoples' needs, change acceptance)
     iv. Establishment of a trust relationship
        (predictable behaviour)

(3)   Other goals

(3.1) Safety – local and community

(3.2) Negotiation

(3.3) Training systems

(3.4) Integration with other (*a*) shifts, (*b*) control centres

It is worth noting that at the same time (1973) the local foremen's association produced a list of objectives for change, including

(*a*) the involvement of supervisors at an early stage in discussions of company changes, e.g. on manning;
(*b*) responsibility for personal assessment of workers;
(*c*) 'we as a group wish to be integrated into the management field';
(*d*) the planning of career possibilities for supervisors, e.g. as deputy managers or staff.

The strategy used

Two different approaches were tried in the Alpha Works. On the 'process' side supervisory and management groups were set up with the support of internal staff consultants, both in the works and for off-site conferences. In the electrical instrument section, however, it was decided to start by getting agreement among managers on the nature of the changes of the supervisory role which would be required. Over a set of meetings, managers came to the conclusion that what they required in this section was the development of the leadership function of supervisors with work teams. They did not want to develop supervisors as assistant managers with 'extensive involvement in problem-solving'.

After this decision supervisors were allowed the same opportunity to go away and discuss their future role with a third-party consultant (an industrial chaplain).

The next stage consisted of a planned 'confrontation' meeting between managers and supervisors, and this was followed by specialist meetings for smaller sections.

In October 1975, a joint working party between the foremen's association and the local management committee reviewed the whole procedure and evaluated progress.

In summary, this was a methods-based strategy (Type IV) which relied on open and honest discussions between parties to uncover the major problems and reach solutions.

The evidence from the cases

The minutes of the joint meeting between the local foremen's association and the site management committee (October 1975) recognized that in spite of the number of meetings 'most of these initiatives had produced little and some degree of frustration had been the result'. There is ample evidence from the notes of various managers and supervisors that many meetings were very difficult.

The first meeting:

'Managers, assistant managers and supervisors – supervisors played their hand very softly. It was very hard to feel how strongly they felt. Often managers were supportive and stronger on behalf of supervisors than the supervisors were themselves. This, apparently, showed a quite different strength of approach than they had voiced in their own private meetings.'

'A number of constructive decisions were made and agreed by all but – managers were fed up with "the watered down" approach of supervisors and supervisors were fed up with their own behaviour. Decision was made to start telling the men and shop stewards what we were doing etc.'

The second meeting:

'Managers, assistant managers and supervisors – met to continue where we left off at the first meeting. Again this was a "gutless" meeting. Problems raised from the supervisors' notes seemed to belong to nobody there, so that we never got to grips with anything. A number of key people were not there – or was it that all problems were passed to absentees? Both managers and supervisors were fed up with lack of trust, frankness etc. General feeling that we should break up into our natural groups and proceed from there – large meetings were just not productive or even meaningful.'

'My own feeling, which took me some time to crystallize, was that only a few supervisors were prepared to attempt real changes in their role without instant increase in pay (these seemed the most capable men anyway). The rest would consider changes if the money came with it – but I suspect they just wanted more money. One or two were just happy as they are now.'

'A dreadful event as far as I was concerned. Contrary to the firm resolve of previous meeting, the majority of supervisors were absolutely passive. Nobody was even openly suspicious of the exercise, or "owned" any of the points in the supervisors' notes. It was generally left to myself and M to represent the supervisors. We both felt a sense of shame at the performance of our colleagues. As far as I could perceive they abdicated their responsibilities to the meeting, and immediately surrendered the initiative to the management group.'

'In spite of this, a lot of work was completed, and targets for some action were set, embracing such topics as manning, mutual response – assessments, documentation, etc., quality of workforce, shop stewards and relationships, supervisor prospects.'

'There was a strong feeling throughout the group that the time must be ripe to begin informing shop stewards, and make them aware of what had been happening. "They must have their suspicions."'

'At the conclusion of this meeting W, G and D felt quite satisfied with the proceedings in comparison to other groups they had been associated with. I had no other experience to relate to, and could only express my despondency at the whole affair.'

'R was very disturbed by the feedback on the meeting after conversation with myself and M. Convened a meeting of supervisors to investigate any reasons for lack of supervisors' involvement.'

However, these reactions are perceptions from within the group process and are highly personal. A more detached view written in August 1974 by a manager who was involved was that the supervisors divided into three groups. One group was very anxious to develop a stronger leadership role; a second group said they were hard worked already and any further responsibility should be accompanied by more pay. A third group merely wanted to be left alone. This manager recognized that some foremen were fairly sceptical about the motives behind the strategy. However, he also argued that other supervisors were actively concerned with the foremen's association, with union negotiations and with developing new job specifications for themselves.

The October 1975 meeting recognized that supervisors should receive more information and would need to improve their relationships with shop stewards.

On the question of career development the report argued that self-development was possible within existing roles; in particular, supervisors should be responsible for assessments on the performance of subordinates and should be involved in selection.

Conclusions

In this case there is little evidence that the strategy tried achieved more than an exchange of views and the possible development of supervisors in group discussion skills. Clearly, a number of useful minor changes were carried through in particular sections, and one of the main consultants in the process claimed in 1976 that there had been certain attitudinal changes among supervisors following the meetings, for example the development of greater tolerance to opposition to improvement plans. 'Supervisors are also now accepted as participants in joint consultative committees.' However, given the types of objectives expressed by management above, it is difficult to avoid the conclusion that the supervisory development programme achieved no major changes whatsoever. The structural problem of the supervisory role created by technical changes and industrial relations pressures could not be changed without more fundamental organizational change.

This example has been given in some detail as it demonstrates some of the difficulties experienced in projects of this type. Fundamentally, the attempt to develop supervisory leadership qualities failed due to:

(a) A lack of motivation on behalf of the supervisors themselves. The management were the main initiators of the change process. Supervisors clearly did not see why they should change their role without fundamental changes in rewards, authority, promotion chances, etc.

(b) This was an attempt to change at the local production system level, whilst leaving the enterprise and the conflictual situations of the business unit's industrial relations exactly where they were. The IR situation defined the interests of the parties involved and these were not changed by reaching 'better understanding'.

(c) The 'process' approach deals with feelings and relationships, but not with performance. There was a need here to specify the levels of performance needed for the whole production system.

(*d*) The approach was too long term in design. If it would have achieved specific improvements and related this to changes in status and reward, the supervisors might have paid more attention.

The TQC (total quality control) approach

The TQC movement stems from a scientific management approach to improving efficiency, but in the development of Japanese company thinking in the 1960s and 1970s this was infused with a concept of 'bottom-up' participative improvements using small groups of employees in 'circles' on a voluntary basis. Supervision, in Japanese factories, stimulated and led these circles, although in Western countries, the experience of quality circles was often seen by supervisors and middle management as a threat (and as so in Sweden by labour unions). The TQC movement, however, did concentrate on system redesign and advocates argued that 85% of faults and malfunctioning were found to be due to the way the system operated, rather than to individual performance errors.

Dr W. Deming makes the following statements on TQC:

'Good quality does not necessarily mean high quality. It means a predictable degree of uniformity and dependability at low cost with a quality suited to the market.'

'Quality cannot be inspected in, it must be built in.'

'Supervision must be designed to help people do a better job.'

'Waste' is defined as follows (Spouster, 1984, pp. 52–3):

— Material waste from faulty equipment
— Machine down-time due to equipment failure
— Slow change-over time in production machinery
— Rework of incorrect goods
— Buffer stocks to protect against delays
— Work in progress due to production schedules
— Long run resulting in high inventory (machine not suitable for demand)
— Warehouse space to store all above
— Confusion between departments
— Clerical errors due to confusion and complexity
— Goods and services not performing to specification
— Poor specifications giving way to inaccurate raw material
— Non-uniform material due to multi-suppliers
— Accounts overdue due to poor documentation
— Poor customer service
— Installation recalls due to faulty installation
— Wrong delivery address

– Wrong goods delivered
– Late or early delivery

The movement for zero defects, total quality control and similar objectives was thus superior to the first two approaches in that it dealt comprehensively with *all* aspects (production-technical, organizational and human) and did try to specify the need for radical redesign of systems. The list of issues given makes this clear. There is considerable attention paid to service management (output efficiency) and to the requirements of 'customers'. TQC in its Japanese form is also anti-expert and stresses the need for everybody in a production system to be involved in system improvement.

Supervision in a TQC approach was intended as a support for improvement: 'Supervision must be designed to help people do a better job.'

There was, however, little new in the TQC approach which helped management to redesign their supervisory systems for such a task. The stated use of 'circles' merely emphasizes the need for worker involvement, and practice varied widely as to how supervision would be associated with such circle activity. Some companies, however, used the circle idea for supervisors themselves. This is a technique which was used in various Scandinavian experiments in the 1970s. It was also found in the Olsen experiment in the UK in the late 1960s on the port installation in the London docks (Thurley and Wirdenius, 1973).

Supervisors met together regularly each week over a 15 month period to plan changes. Experiments carried out by ANCO in the 1970s followed a similar approach (Lyons, 1976).

In general terms, therefore, the improvement of supervisory management performance requires a far more radical and comprehensive strategy than that found in these four contrasting approaches. Such an improvement requires overall restructuring of the relationships of supervisors together with functional specialists and management itself. European supervisory systems are deeply entrenched in existing organizational relationships and behaviour; small changes are not enough.

7.4 Directions of change: a diagnostic experiment

In 1979, the authors were involved with Tom Lyons of the Irish Productivity Centre in an experiment in Ireland in diagnosing the directions of change required in seven factories. The framework used for the diagnosis is given in the Appendix. The experiment involved sending teams of international supervisory experts to the factories which were owned by a number of different nationalities. The teams produced a range of different solutions.

The Kilkea project (Lyons, 1981)

(a) Using a Type III strategy (rational) involving external specialists observing seven organizations it was found that each case was highly specific. Therefore the recommendations for change were different in each case. Seven different teams produced seven different solutions. The case clearly demonstrated the need for recommendations to be tailor-made for each individual company situation (not following a standard prescription).

(b) The majority of recommendations at the operational level indicated the need to make organizational changes rather than to rely on traditional training solutions for individuals.

(c) In general terms, the different teams thought that more involvement for supervisors was needed at the operational level (which meant upgrading supervision). They also pointed to the need for redesigning the supervisory role.

The major recommendations of the project teams can be seen in Table 7.1.

The classification of factories used the Joan Woodward system of distinguishing production systems by the extent to which they could be seen as a mass production standardized operation, a batch production system or a system involving 'process' technology.

The recommendations could be classified in terms of:

(a) Decentralizing decisions so that supervisory management systems have greater control and autonomy. The precise functions and roles involved clearly vary with the type of production system, e.g. planning is more important for batch production.

(b) Developing the technical improvement role for supervisors. Differences between the cases also reflected the overall history and culture of the plant, i.e. technology was not the only set of variables affecting the actual need for change.

The cases demonstrated the need for making a systematic appraisal of the actual roles of supervisiors as a basis for radically restructuring supervisory management. This leads to the need for an overall approach.

Type of production system	Organizational changes				Industrial training/development			
	Involve supervisors in mgt decisions	Delegate authority to supervisors	Involve supervisors in control systems	Involve supervisors in planning	Technical knowledge	Disturbance handling	Industrial relations	Human relations, leadership
Mass	•	•						
Mass	•					•	•	•
Mass	•	•				•		
Process, batch	•		•		•	•	•	
Process, small batch					•			
Batch	•	•	•	•	•			•
Batch			•	•				

Table 7.1 Major recommendations of the project teams.

7.5 An overall approach for regenerating supervisory management

Objectives of change

(*a*) Taking production activities seriously means advocating a process by which all 'production systems' – in manufacturing, service and research activities – need to be re-examined continuously in terms of their effectiveness.

(*b*) The criteria for measuring effectiveness should be comprehensive, i.e. dealing with input efficiency, system efficiency and output efficiency.

(*c*) In organizational terms, it is impossible to envisage a single model which is functional for the whole range of types of production systems.

Table 7.2 illustrates this by showing some of the very different organizational problems created for different types of production system.

Bench-mark system	Organizational needs
Mass production (assembly line)	Large-scale standardized control
Building construction	Flexible tailor-made decision-making
Mass production (non-line)	Co-ordination of component supply
Small batch manufacture	Planning and co-ordination
Process production	Effective integration of activities
Transport control	Fast centralized resource allocation
Medium/large batch manufacture	Production control and quality control
Supermarket (retail)	Customer service and standard controls
Computerized administration (office)	Integration and availability of data
Hospital emergency service	Flexible fast service
Container transport	Long-term planning of system activities
Mining	Planning and flexible responses
Forestry	Control over decentralized activities
Engineering maintenance	Co-ordination between production and maintenance
Building maintenance	Motivation of long-term planned activities

Table 7.2 *Types of production system and their organizational implications.*

(*d*) Some general principles, however, can be stated:

(*i*) A production system is best organized as a discrete system with clear collective responsibility defined for running the system among the supervisory managers. Organizational autonomy is necessary.

(*ii*) All managers in the system should be encouraged to be oriented towards technological improvements, i.e a strong 'technical' orientation is essential (even in service organizations).

(*iii*) Promotion, status and reward systems need to be designed to allow managers of high qualifications and intelligence and extensive work experience to be concerned with the improvement of production system efficiencies. (This principle implies that supervisory management needs to include a mix of junior and senior staff. The latter should be rewarded according to their status and functional usefulness, so that it should be commonplace for senior managers to be working within supervisory management for temporary periods even at the end of their careers.)

(e) QWL objectives (satisfaction etc.) and TQC objectives (raising quality standards) and service management objectives (taking customer needs seriously) all need to be pursued by supervisory management and balanced accordingly. In particular, top management may need to be reminded that the commitment of employees to production system objectives will depend on the acceptance of the objectives as legitimate and on the perceived justice of the arrangements governing employee work. Essentially a *European* approach means a balance between system effectiveness and employee needs and demands.

A suggested strategy for change

A successful approach needs to be comprehensive, long term and ultimately radical in its implications. It is likely to be complex in that different strategies for change will have to be used at different stages. A general model of such an overall approach is given in Fig. 7.2. An example of a detailed diagnostic approach is given in the Appendix.

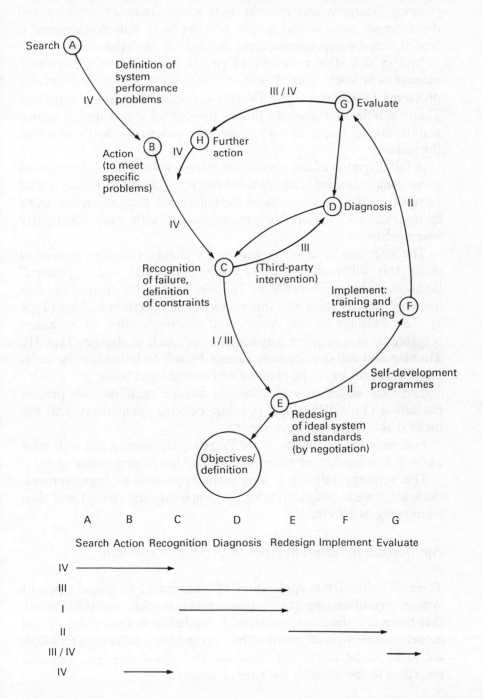

Search (A)

Definition of
system
performance
problems

IV

III / IV

(G) Evaluate

(B)   IV   (H) Further
action

Action
(to meet
specific
problems)

IV

(D) Diagnosis

II

III

Recognition
of failure,
definition
of constraints

(C) (Third-party
intervention)

Implement:
training and
restructuring (F)

I / III

Self-development
programmes

II

(E)

Redesign
of ideal system
and standards
(by negotiation)

Objectives/
definition

A   B   C   D   E   F   G

Search Action Recognition Diagnosis Redesign Implement Evaluate

IV   ⟶

III   ⟶

I   ⟶

II   ⟶

III / IV   ⟶

IV   ⟶

Figure 7.2 *The redesign of production system supervisory management.*

Note that this approach includes problem definition, recognition of failures, diagnosis and experimental action, redesign, training and development and evaluation. The philosophy of self- development is crucial. Step-by-step improvement depends on this orientation.

In Fig. 7.2, the redesign of production system supervisory management starts from A with the analysis of system performance problems by using a Type IV (group/circle discussion) approach. There is little alternative to this as the crucial knowledge of system malfunctioning is usually only really fully understood by those within the system.

A full diagnosis of the reasons for system failure, however, requires more comprehensive study by third parties – specialist research. Full recognition at C of the reasons for failure will depend on the active co-operation of supervisory management with such third-party investigators.

The next step is to set objectives for change (E). The process of doing this will require further study (Type III) and a 'political' decision, either unilaterally or by negotiation. All change involves losses as well as gains and this requires such decision-making (Type I). The redesign of the system and the implication of a change programme also requires a systematic approach to change (Type II). Training and self-development cannot be left to individual choice as the new system has to be planned and brought into being.

The final stages of evaluating the change requires both process evaluation (Type III) and, if possible, external comparison. This will mean that a further study is needed.

Following the evaluation, Type IV group discussions can start once again in locating further system failure and the process starts again.

The strategy implies a long-term approach to improvement, changing system design, training and implementing change and then monitoring its effects.

Application to different types of production system

Table 7.3 shows the application of this model to three types of system: manufacturing (batch production), service and R&D. Note that there are significant differences needed in following the overall model in each type of system. The only golden rule here is to follow the logic of the model but think out the actual strategies required according to the needs of the type of system.

7.6 Conclusions

Taking production seriously is a radical step for many organizations in Western Europe. Since the explosion of European culture in the sixteenth and seventeenth centuries and the vast technological improvements of the nineteenth and twentieth centuries there has been a steady decline in the relative status and importance of those concerned with 'production' efficiency. This has to be reversed. The details of production efficiency in a world of high technology are crucial and require systematic and creative thought for success.

It follows that a new vision is necessary of the world of 'production'. Creativity is an essential value of European society. If 'production' is seen as the realm of the standardized control system, then it is easily perceived as a cold and dead world for professionals and intellectuals. The world of supervisory management is then a very dull world indeed. The American and Japanese approaches both tend to present, for example, TQC in this light. The argument here is that there is on the contrary an essentially creative element in supervisory management and that this creativity needs to be recognized and rewarded.

A final essential element is that of involvement and participation. The essence of democracy is that recognition is given to the interests of all elements in society, especially to those who are seen as occupying low status positions. This principle, according to A. D. Lindsey (1943), is best expressed as 'The wearer knows where the shoe fits.'

Those involved in production know best where the shoe fits. It is important therefore to plan supervisory systems which involve all those who have to work within each production system. This does not mean the abolition of 'supervision', but the strengthening and recognition of the function.

	Manufacturing (batch)	Service	R & D
A Search	IV Quality circle groups review performance and quality failures	III Customer needs survey	IV Professional project teams study of possible innovatory areas
B Action	IV Supervisory action to remedy faulty operations	IV Supervisory action to improve customer service	IV Experimentation in product development
C Recognition	III Measurement of performance data and failures (third-party help)	III Measurement of sales and service satisfaction and shortfalls (third-party help)	IV Study of comparative advantage of innovation
D Diagnosis	IV Identification of causes of failure	IV Identification of causes of failure	III Identification of organizational context of failure

Table 7.3 Application of redesign model on three types of production system.

	Manufacturing (batch)	Service	R & D
E Redesign	I Negotiation for system redesign (unions and functional departments)	I Redesign organization for specialist service	IV Redesign organization (multi-project groups) I (negotiate)
F Implementation	II Implement education and training programmes (self-development)	II Retrain, select new staff for roles	II Systematic implementation of organization and human resource development
G Evaluation	III/IV Double evaluation (process) and system performance	III/IV Double evaluation (short and long)	III System evaluation
H Action	IV Supervisory teams restructured to implement further actions	IV Restudy of customer needs	IV Restudy of new areas

Table 7.3 continued

8 The European answer: conditions for success

8.1 The long march

Three issues have dominated our discussions and each one has presented a formidable intellectual challenge over more than a decade of debate, research and experimentation. Most fundamentally, there is the question of improving and restructuring the economic systems of Western Europe to meet enhanced competition from North America, Japan and the Far Eastern NICS and other rapidly developing economic powers. There is little disagreement on the necessity, but much on the direction and process of change which this entails. Secondly, we have devoted much of our analysis to the issue of how to provide a new framework and identity for the managerial systems for European firms. The implication here is that such managerial reform is a condition for economic revitalization. The third issue then follows: how to take practical steps towards such a managerial revolution. A single strategy or set of prescriptions are unlikely to prove relevant to many firms, as there is such a huge range of different organizational and cultural situations.

It is only by the close of the 1980s that it has become clear that solutions for each of these issues are interconnected. This poses considerable problems for most Europeans who are instinctively sceptical of grand solutions and ideological answers. The 'long march' of European integration since the Second World War has been a step-by-step affair, with many halts at apparently intractable problems. Success in the political and economic spheres has only come from patient negotiation, often in the midst of crisis. The dominant mood, even in countries with socialist governments, is distrust of government and bureaucratic arrangements and scepticism about social planning. It is believed that individuals at the operational level, who have first-hand experience of actual problems and difficulties, should be given freedom to take decisions about organizational and personal matters. How then can one support an approach which argues for a coherent, even if varied, set of strategies of change leading to managerial and organizational reform? Will this not lead back to the arid generalizations and slogans now seen as characteristic of European socialism in at least most of its forms?

We will argue here that the 'long march' of European integration will continue and must include managerial reform. The pressures for liberalizing trade are clear enough and this leads to the creation of trans-European firms operating across borders. At this point, national and traditional company practices will be found to be inadequate and inefficient. The demand for a managerial revolution starts here. The creation of effective trans-European organizations requires new managerial systems which will receive legitimacy and support only if they are rooted in the values and behaviour of a European way of life. Our argument for 'European Management' inevitably requires thinking out the conditions under which this is possible. It also involves accepting the need for comprehensive and radical change.

The military threat to Western Europe since the Second World War has come from the East; the more recent economic threat comes from the 'Pacific Alliance' of North American high technology multinationals with Asian firms, particularly Japanese. Much has been written on the 'Japanese miracle' and a great deal can be heavily discounted as based on myth and half-truths. It is, however, of the greatest importance to Europeans not to underestimate the extent to which American expertise in production engineering was tranferred to Japan and has now been re-exported back to the United States in an improved form, as well as diffused to Korea, Taiwan and other Asian countries. The essential point here is that mass secondary education, combined with a philosophy of mass scientific management – by which all employees attempt to improve the effectiveness of the production process and the quality of the product – transforms the competitive edge of manufacturing by reducing costs and improving the product. The introduction of automation and new technology only yields real results where the employees running the plant have the education to understand the potentialities of the new machinery and the motivation to exploit this to the full. The motivation comes from a social structure where there is enough openness to persuade individuals that 'self-development' is the main way for career achievement. In spite of the traditional authority structures of Asian societies, it is clear that it is possible to achieve this 'openness', especially in new factories in new industries. Much of this has been achieved by learning from American human resource development thinking.

We have emphasized the historical context of much of the typical European traditional production organization arrangements. Crafts and specialist professional technical occupations have created organizations in which the main function seems to be to protect the identity of the individual. Mass production is still seen by intellectuals as a deskilling process and the enemy of creativity. Scientific management is the tool of the specialist engineer or manager. Industrial relations is the field of collective bargaining by which the shop stewards or interest group representatives regulate the rewards of their constituent members. All this reduces the motivation of those at all levels in improving the effectiveness of the process or the quality of the product.

Manufacturing effectiveness is, however, only the beginning of the challenge. In spite of the public emphasis on the visible trade balance, the battle for the 1990s is shifting to science and technology. European science and technology, with all its glittering set of Nobel prizes and scholarly achievements, is no longer at the centre of most scientific fields. Where are the European super computors? Why does Europe have such little expertise in microprocessors and in computor storage devices? How far do European firms still have a lead in biotechnology? Where is the European R&D lead in photographic technology now after the onslaught from Japan?

Pessimism about European science and technology can be easily exaggerated, of course, and there are many contrary success stories. Nevertheless, there is at least a half-truth in the image projected by many West Coast American business and political leaders – echoed frequently in Japan – of a European society, which is rich and complacent, dominated by holidays, leisure pursuits, the contemplation of a rich cultural heritage and the protection of the environment. Science and technology, since the atomic bomb, have changed from being the guarantee for human progress to the source of possible human destruction. There is increasing evidence that such fears are behind the decline of the attractiveness of natural science and technology as specialisms at university.

Much public debate within Europe concentrates on the failure of firms to translate scientific discoveries into usable commercial products, certainly compared with Japan and the United States. If true, this is clearly a failure of management organization and policy. In the 1950s, Tom Burns and George Stalker (1961), carried out their classic investigation into the Scottish electronics industry, focusing on the social and 'political' factors which lay behind the failure to adapt from defence industry work to consumer and market-oriented product development. Their argument was that firms were dominated by rigid hierarchical organizations, where the R&D departments were segregated away from production and marketing. This argument has been repeated by McKinsey in a recent report on the UK electronics industry (NEDO, 1988).

Such hierarchies insulate top management from knowledge of the realities of customer needs or scientific potential. They also frustrate the specialists within R&D and marketing.

The challenge to European electronics firms comes first from the American information technology companies. IBM represents one form of this challenge, Apple and Digital another. Both emphasize the individual, freedom of action for top management, rewards for individuals who follow the 'enterprise culture' and total commitment to corporate goals. Both emphasize the need for total flexibility and willingness to learn to do any job. IBM offers employment security, not job security, within a strong corporate culture, with much regulation of employee behaviour. Apple and other Californian firms offer large responsibilities and rewards to young graduates, who may decide to leave after a relatively short career within the company. The dominant values are the fast self-development of the individual in a society where competitiveness is supreme. Taxation and public social security are ideally seen as minimal; economic decisions, freely taken should be prior to political and social regulation. Education should be pragmatic and vocationally oriented. Individuals should pay for their own training (Becker, 1975). Business strategy, closely related to customer need (Peters and Waterman, 1982), is the crucial rationality behind progress.

The Japanese challenge is more subtle. There are many similar aspects to the American firms. Flexibility and total corporate commitment are crucial. Self-development is also the dominant process of human resource development, but within a collectivist framework of peer group pressures. Competition exists for the individual, because of this framework. Attention to customer need and service management are constantly emphasized. What is different about the Japanese challenge was shown vividly in a recent speech by Mr Takeshita, then Japanese Prime Minister, at the Mansion House in London (May, 1988). He argued that Japan would now place cultural and scientific relations and exchanges as their most important international objective. The Japanese see scientific and technological progress as the basis for a knowledge-based 'high tech' society. This means establishing an international set of R&D institutions. It has to be based on political partnership between USA, Europe and Japan. Japan aims to infiltrate and influence European thinking towards supporting a global 'high tech' society. Economic decision-making comes after these objectives. Companies will retain identity and loyalty around a key cadre of scientists and engineers. Product development is the crucial process behind competitive power. Organization has to be flexible and project teams must retain total commitment. Work remains dominant and prior to leisure, for all key company members.

The European rallying cry, 1992, takes place in the face of such competition. American, Japanese and many other Far Eastern countries' firms are already established within the European Community. The breaking down of barriers and the expansion of markets also benefits such firms. At the same time, European firms are investing heavily in and buying into North American, and to a much lesser extent, Japanese based companies. How far can the managements of Siemens and Philips, Fiat and Volkswagen, Renault and GEC, etc., build world empires effectively, without clear managerial philosophies which motivate their employees to work for a European as opposed to an American or Japanese firm? The 'long march' of European integration will be worthless, if it results in a common market dominated by foreign firms.

8.2 Continuity and innovation

We have followed, in our analysis, the argument of Harbison and Myers (1959) that management consists of three interlocking aspects: an authority system, a technical resource and a status system. If the status system is regarded as outdated and unjust then managerial authority will be challenged. If managers are seen as possessing little technical knowledge, they will be dismissed as irrelevant. If the authority system decays, then management cannot use their technical expertise. How far are European managements suffering from such problems?

Our review of management at the operational, middle management and enterprise levels supports the view that there is a long-term structural decay in the viability of management within European firms. There are eight reasons for this judgement:

(a) Traditional status systems are in decline, but it has been difficult to replace them with a new legitimate élite. This is largely the result of changes in the higher educational systems of West European countries. *Grandes écoles* and prestigious universities have suffered severe competition from newer universities, but business schools have had only a limited succes in developing an MBA élite. (The mass production of MBAs, now contemplated in the UK, seems likely only to debase the qualification. In Sweden this debasement may have occurred already, judging from the serious criticism recently levelled against economist training at universities.) Professional qualifications are supposed to be mutually recognized by EC member states after 1992, but given the different validation processes in each country, it will be difficult to achieve a Europewide system of professional technical qualifications for managerial specialists.

(b) Large companies suffer from rigid hierarchies (see above) which isolate top management, confine middle management (the term used in a general sense) to administrative roles and frustrate operational and supervisory management in their decision-making.

There are many changes taking place, in large companies, to counter this problem. Profit centres and divisional organization are the most commonly used systems. However, it is not easy to 'debureaucratize' an organization, even by using the pressures of the market. Career systems are the root of the problem. Careers have to be provided, even if the traditional hierarchy is abolished. This clearly means a need for more specialist career routes.

(c) Top management has severe problems in developing strategic planning which commands the respect of middle and lower management.

The theory of strategic choice is well understood among top management, particularly if they have had American business school training. The problem lies in developing such plans and getting them accepted both at board level and throughout the organization. This is a problem again of organization. Valid planning requires inputs from operational and middle management and needs project organization to develop such ideas. It is not easy to use projects for senior management decision-making.

(d) Specialist functional divisions within management are often based on specialist occupational careers and qualifications. Such divisions reflect different subcultures and values and provide a breeding ground for 'political warfare'.

Conflicts between finance departments, R & D and personnel are legion. The growth of company-wide information systems demands close integration of objectives for effectiveness, but the social and cultural roots of specialization go back to early choices within the educational system. Demands for professional job autonomy exacerbate this problem.

(e) Traditional internal labour market careers for managers in large firms is now being replaced by headhunters and Sunday newspaper advertisements. Mid-career development courses are used to change jobs. The problem here is that the new mobility is highly dysfunctional if firms have inadequate methods for assessing the types of managerial positions really required and for assessing those on the market for new jobs. Senior management development programmes need to be integrated with recruitment programmes for this purpose.

(f) Organizational learning is poorly developed in European firms. This is because learning is still seen as an individual process, particularly for young graduate trainees. Given the depth and variety of subcultures within firms and the differences in behaviour and thinking between European countries, European managers need a great deal of conceptual flexibility and a capacity for cultural empathy in order to understand each other. This is also a question of language skills, combined with interpersonal and problem-solving skills. Above all there has to be a capacity for system thinking and a motivation to transmit knowledge to subordinates and peers.

(g) Creativity is widely praised in intellectuals in European society, but is not seen as a key attribute for management. Koestler (1975) argued that creativity needs a capacity to respond to uncertainty and discontinuity. This would seem to be essential for designing a strategic response following a contingency or a disaster. Behind this point is the gap in European society still between the 'cultured' professional and the manager. If managers see themselves as cultural 'philistines', as agents of an organization and not as creative persons, and if creativity is not rewarded through appraisal, then it is difficult to expect intelligent responses and brilliant combinations of scientific and marketing thinking. Product development, in these circumstances, will be merely routine.

(h) Effective leadership in European firms is too often seen as the product of the strong and arbitrary individual. The long development and debate on participation, co-determination and industrial democracy has not weakened such views. On the contrary, as participation is associated with time-wasting committees, managerial leadership is associated with knowing what to do and 'going after it'. Participation, however, requires the involvement of all levels and interest groups in deciding policy and strategy and certainly requires new institutions to allow this to happen (Thurley, 1988). The argument of Wilfred Brown in the Glacier Metal experiment (1960) is still valid. Effective management is only possible when there is real consent to managerial policies among all levels of employees.

Continuity requires managers to be aware of the past. Their actions have to use symbols which utilize traditional values and ideas. Management in an enterprise is not in a vacuum. All the employees and customers, etc., also belong to communities, which in the European case are very diverse. Continuity therefore means connecting to those different communities.

Innovation has to be sought by following through from continuity. There are many new groups which are not satisfied with traditional values and standards. Innovation means a focus on the future and its possibilities. Our argument here is that a new and viable European management style and philosophy would be able to point to the future, whilst retaining responsibility for protecting selected aspects of the past.

8.3 Choices

Management is about steering enterprises and production systems, sometimes in calm and predictable circumstances and sometimes in the teeth of a gale of events which are completely unpredicted. Essentially, there needs to be a set of maps, an objective and a planned route, plus a compass and a system of checking position and how far off the planned route the organization has strayed.

Organizational maps are of two types: those that point to the policies (or sets of policies) that could be attempted and those that analyse the processes that could be used. The former are based on rational classifications and typologies, the latter on models of action and causation of effects within organizational entities.

Our first map for the European manager tries to depict the policy choices for organizations that are trying to balance interest group needs against the requirements of running an integrated controlled and effective organizational system. This could be seen as a trade-off between industrial relations objectives and production engineering and systems engineering objectives. In Fig. 8.1, one dimension, the vertical, refers to the degree to which interest groups are recognized and their different objectives dealt with. The horizontal dimension refers to the extent to which individual managerial discretion is merged into an overall system of control, with specified limits of autonomy.

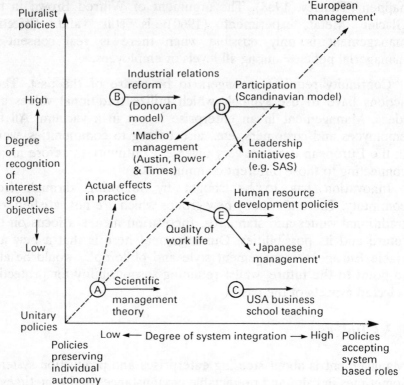

Figure 8.1 *Policy choices for European managers.*

The degree of pluralism accepted by enterprise managements varies, of course, considerably between different nation states within Western Europe, different product markets and industries, different states of the labour market and the relative sophistication of the personnel management policies and practices adopted by the enterprise. It is also important to underline the fact that 'pluralism' is an interactive relationship and not simply a description of the 'political' situation. This means that an important factor is the attitude and stance of the labour movement, at all its levels of operation. Choices of strategy for managements, therefore, start with their diagnosis of where they are on the vertical axis and where, given social and political trends, they want to go. The debate on participation within Europe makes it plain that senior managements are deeply divided on their objectives in this respect. The extent to which enterprises and production systems are run in a tightly controlled and integrated fashion is also highly variable.

This reflects technological requirements, the demands of customers and management style. In general terms, automation leads to tightly controlled systems, but the design of enterprise organization could be planned around the notion of a type of federation of systems or alternatively, around the concept of a single integrated system. Choice of strategy here therefore means that managements have to reflect on their existing structures and systems of control and how far these have to be changed.

Figure 8.1 shows the influence of several contemporary arguments on the choices available to management. The overall direction of change for European managers is clear enough. What needs to be emphasized here is that at the enterprise level this can mean very different strategies being adopted.

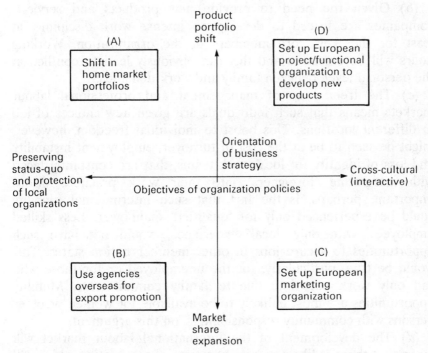

Figure 8.2 *Policy choices for internationalization strategies.*

Figure 8.2 shows the choices available to managements that are pursuing a strategy of internationalization. Here the crucial dimensions of choice are the extent to which a strategy has to be based on marketing requirements or technological demands and the extent to which it is seen as desirable to maintain local cultural identities or, alternatively, to build a new cross-cultural and integrated organizational identity. The focus of four alternative strategies are given as examples of this choice. It needs to be emphasized that 1992 does not necessarily mean the growth of giant trans-national corporations. A more effective approach may well lie in preserving the current effectiveness of locally based firms, but developing a more international marketing strategy.

The crucial nature of such choices for firms facing the creation of a single product and labour market across the European Community cannot be exaggerated. One extreme scenario for the effects of 1992, for example, could be that:

(a) Large corporations move into the current national markets and take over smaller national and regional companies. This could lead to conflicts between such firms and local communities, as displayed in the recent Nestlé/Rowntree case.

(b) Given the need to provide new products and services, companies are forced to develop an intense work discipline, at least for the 'key' core members of the organization. Working hours will be extended and this can obviously lead to conflict, at the personal level, between family and work demands.

(c) The freeing up of management and professional labour markets means that such individuals are given new choices of job in different locations. This boost to individual freedom, however, might be seen to be at the cost of turnover, employment instability and loss of identity for local work teams, that are constantly faced with integrating 'foreigners' into their work practices. More important, perhaps, is the fact that such international mobility could be experienced only for 'qualified' manpower. Less skilled employees, with only 'local' experience, would not have such opportunities to secure jobs in other member nation states. This would be true, particularly, for the unemployed or for those who can only work part-time due to family commitments. Mobility opportunities are most unlikely to be available for women or older persons with community responsibilities, on this argument.

(d) The development of the international labour market will mean that there is likely to be a new type of segregation which will be reflected in salary levels. The 'international' levels of salary for managers and professionals leads to a severe rise in house prices in the 'metropolitan' areas and social conflicts with the local employees who are paid much less and cannot any longer afford to remain in the major cities. This appears to be the situation already in the new developments now under way in the City of London and the new Docklands area.

Such a scenario is possible, but could be avoided. The influence of basic philosophies on managerial thinking may be critical in determining what will actually happen. If the 'new individualism' of the radical right triumphs, then Europe could indeed be transformed into a 'Californian style' society, where individual freedom and autonomy are dominant values. A triumph for Japanese ideas might well mean a boost for scientific and technological research and the growth of Japanese/American collaboration around scientific institutes and large R&D centres. Corporations might try to become the focus for the identity of their employees and this could be successful, at least for younger employees, under certain conditions. Management, under Japanese influence, would certainly try to influence employees towards a greater degree of co-operation with each other and a greater sense of service management. They could, however, be drawn into conflict with local communities, due to the severe nature of demands on individual commitment.

We are assuming here that both these scenarios are unlikely to prove acceptable. This then leads to the case for a third alternative: European management, which is described and summarized below.

8.4 The European management model

In our discussions, we have indicated the type of assumptions and strategies which might categorize an approach to management which is peculiarly and distinctly European. It is useful to bring together the major characteristics of this approach at this point.

Assumptions

Six needs or values could be said to provide the major starting points for managerial action:

(a) The need for scientific, rational thinking to guide decisions.

(b) The need for managers to evolve specific pragmatic strategies suited to the precise situation, rather than following universalistic theories or solutions based on ideologies. (This need leads to the necessity of rational choice based on diagnosis and sober assessment of alternative strategies.)

(c) The need for emotional commitment to making a change initiative work. This implies inspiring employees to take future possibilities seriously.

(*d*) The need to utilize managerial and technical experience – and the judgements based on this – to the fullest degree. Social capital is composed of such learnt behaviour, skills and knowledge. Even granted that such experience may have led to narrow and prejudiced judgements and biases, given open debate and a scientific philosophy (Popper, 1963), they are the best basis for rational thinking.

(*e*) The need to accept a 'pluralist' view of the enterprise which combines the necessity of achieving commitment to organizational goals and a democratic process for arriving at broadly consensual decisions.

(*f*) The need for creative learning, through and with other colleagues, together with self-development, as a continuous process within organizational work life. Such learning has to be a continuation of the educational process, for all ages and for all levels.

Policy objectives

These assumptions can be argued to lead to a number of policy objectives:

(*a*) Build the best possible interpersonal human relationships. Excellent performance is possible without such relationships being established, but it is difficult to maintain in the long run. As Elton Mayo argued, however, the creation of excellent human relations at work is crucial for personal happiness and avoiding discord and anomie in the community at large. It is therefore a social goal in its own right.

(*b*) Establish open channels for dialogue between all parties involved in the work situation. Participation is also an end in itself in a democratic society, as well as a sensible process for tapping the ideas and knowledge of all employees.

(*c*) Provide a work situation in which identity is both individual and collective. The task situation should be meaningful for the individual, but also the historical context in which it is placed. (The St Crispin's speech of Henry V, in the Shakespearen play, expresses this well.)

(*d*) Involve all employees in improving standards, suggesting innovations and improving quality. This should also be an end in itself and not simply for organizational competitive purposes, as may happen in Japanese cases.

(*e*) Create new reward systems based on individual autonomy and individual needs. This means the acceptance of greater inequality between individuals, but the rules governing rewards have to be open, democratically discussed and rigorously applied.

(*f*) Focus system design on the acceptance of key, selected and mutually agreed performance standards.

(*g*) Collective bargaining should be focused on the negotiation of minimal employees' rights in the work situation.

(*h*) Provide new procedures and institutions for the settlement of disputes without the use of power by either side.

(*i*) Provide a new policy for selecting managers and technical specialists on the grounds of merit, from all levels of employees, providing appropriate training and education. This would lead to opening up management selection to women and disadvantaged groups.

(*j*) Provide resources and opportunities for continuous self-development for all levels.

(*k*) Secure the active support of community and other local groups for managerial objectives. This means that the conflict for employees between work commitments and private life has to be openly negotiated.

(*l*) Concentrate scientific and technological research and development of products on long-term and mutually agreed objectives and provide a mass technological educational programme to allow this to happen.

(*m*) Develop managerial decision-making in as open a manner as possible, utilizing third-party consultants and researchers and regularly reporting to employees on progress.

(*n*) Develop and constantly reappraise visions for the future. To see ahead is crucial, but most predictions are likely to be wrong.

The creation of managerial legitimacy

Such objectives can be seen as the basis of a possible consensus agreement – either formally or informally – which could provide the essential legitimacy to allow managers to act decisively and effectively. The essential difference between the European and the American and Japanese approaches to management lies in the fact that, for many Europeans, the legitimacy of management in both the private and the public sector has to be created. Most American conceptualizations of managerial efficiency concentrate on the importance of strategy formulation, systems of control, customer service and marketing policies, human resource development, etc. It is not considered that there is a prior problem of creating a legitimate role for managers. The Japanese case is similar. The assumption is that given the policies of life time commitment and enterprise unionism, Japanese employees will give their loyalty to the enterprise. In European society, with all its history of class struggle and revolution, the belief was that socialism would allow organizations to be planned rationally and run effectively. We now know that in state socialist countries, such a dream was naive. Even in social democratic countries, the nationalization of enterprises did not solve this problem (although it did allow rationalization). Wilfred Brown (1960) in his Glacier Metal experiment in the UK did see the issue clearly, forty years ago, although his solution – to turn enterprises into 'democratic states' – was not effective.

Our argument here is therefore that managerial legitimacy can only be created and maintained if the objectives of the organization continue to command the support of the various interest groups within it. Such a consensus has to be continually fought for: it will be eroded over time if there are not adjustments to the demands of new interest groups.

If legitimacy can be assumed by managers, then their power is greatly enhanced. It will be possible to move quickly in emergencies and to plan decisive strategies of product development to guarantee survival against competition.

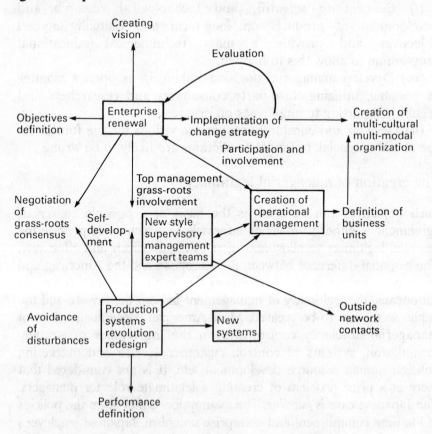

Figure 8.3 *European management: Model of strategic change.*

A model of strategic change

Management needs to be understood as a multi-level problem. We have distinguished three levels conceptually: enterprise management, operational management and supervisory management. Figure 8.3 takes these three levels and shows the basic actions which must be carried out to provide the renewal of an enterprise. This is therefore a model of strategic change.

8.5 On being a European manager

In redefining the concept of management, we are implicitly changing the nature of managerial roles. The term 'management' is profoundly unsatisfactory as it is an umbrella term for different types of roles and activities. Given our approach, therefore, what jobs would European managers be actually doing?

There are five roles which seem to be the most critical (see Fig. 8.4). At the beginning of a career, managers should be students (A), not only in the formal sense, but in the general meaning of focusing on learning from experience. As argued above, managers should be drawn from many sources and levels. The role, however, is to learn about organizational life in as comprehensive a manner as possible. The second role is that of a functional staff specialist (B). Here the focus is on information gathering and analysis. This is the scientific role, essential for effective decision-making. The third role is that of supervisory management (C). Here the focus is on making systems work and on solving problems of disturbances to planned performance. The fourth role is that of the operational manager (D). Here, the role focuses on the interrelationships between economic, technical, social and political objectives. The final role is that of top mangement (E). Here the focus must be on vision, commitment and essential cultural innovations.

Figure 8.4 shows these roles in the form of an ideal career path for a European executive. Such a career is likely to be both within and between different organizations, probably located in different countries. Ideally, a balance has to be struck between developing managers by rotating them between posts inside an organization and planning for external mobility and (occasional) changes of employer.

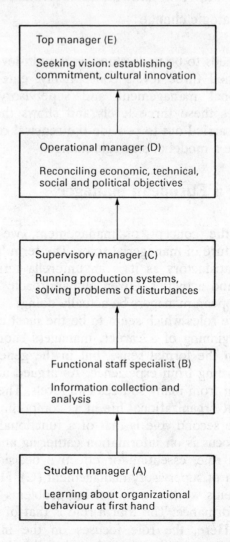

Figure 8.4 *Career path for a European manager.*

Essentially, however, the dominant philosophy must still be that learnt from the ancient Greeks – that balance is crucial between the competing obligations that civilized persons must recognize as inescapable. The vision must be that Europeans can offer a new and richer approach to management where economic and business goals can be pursued within commitments to political and cultural life.

References

Abegglen, J. (1957) *The Japanese Factory*. Free Press, Glencoe, Illinois.

Ansoff, T.H. (1965) *Corporate Strategy*. McGraw-Hill, New York.

Argyris, C. and Schön, D. (1978) *Organizational Learning*. Addison-Wesley, Reading, Massachusetts.

Bakke, E.W. (1966) *Bonds of Organization*. Archon Books, Hamden, Connecticut.

Barnard, C.I. (1947) *Functions of the Executive*. Oxford University Press, Oxford.

Barnett, C. (1986) *The Audit of War: The Illusion and Reality of Britain as a Great Nation*. Macmillan, London.

Basset, P. (1987) *Strike Free: New Industrial Relations in Britain*. Macmillan, London.

Beckard, R. (1969) *Organization Development: Strategies and Models*. Addison-Wesley, Reading, Massachusetts.

Becker, G.S. (1975) *Human Capital*. University of Chicago Press, Chicago.

Beckérus, Å. and Edström, A. (eds) (1988) *Doktrinskiftet: Nya ideal i svenskt ledarskap*. (In Swedish), (The doctrine shift: New ideals in Swedish leadership.) Svenska Dagbladet, Stockholm.

Bennis, W.G. (1966) *Changing Organizations: Essays on the Development and Evolution of Human Organization.* McGraw-Hill, New York.

Bingham, W.V. (1937) *Aptitudes and Aptitude Testing.* Harper, New York.

Blake, R.R. (1969) *Grid Organizational Development.* Addison-Wesley, New York.

Blake, R.R. and Mouton, J.S. (1985) *The Managerial Grid III.* Gulf Publishing, Houston.

Blanchard, K.H. and Johnson, S. (1982) *The One-Minute Manager.* Morrow, New York.

Boddewyn, J.J. (ed.)(1976) *European Industrial Managers.* Industrial Arts and Science Press.

Brooke, M.Z. (1987) *International Management: A Review of Strategies and Opportunities.* Hutchinson, London.

Brown, W. (1960) *Exploration in Management.* Heinemann, London.

Burns, T. (1957) Management in action. *Operational Research Quarterly,* **8**:45–60.

Burns, T. and Stalker, G.M. (1961) *The Management of Innovation.* Tavistock, London.

Carlson, S. (1951) *Executive Behaviour: A Study of the Work Load and the Working Methods of Managing Directors.* Strömbergs, Stockholm.

Cartwright, D. and Zander, A. (eds)(1960) *Group Dynamics.* Harper & Row, New York.

Chandler, A.D.,Jr (1962) *Strategy and Structure: Chapters in the History of the American Industrial Enterprise.* MIT Press, Cambridge, Massachusetts.

Child, J. (1969) *British Management Thought*. George Allen and Unwin, London

Cole, R. (1979) *Work, Mobility and Participation: A Comparative Study of American and Japanese Industry*. University of California Press, California.

Crozier, M. (1964) *The Bureaucratic Phenomenon*. University of Chicago Press, Chicago and London.

Cyert, R.M. and March, J.G. (1966) *A Behavioral Theory of the Firm*. Prentice Hall, Englewood Cliffs, New Jersey.

Dahrendorf, R. (1959) *Class and Class Conflict in an Industrial Society*. Routledge and Kegan Paul, London.

Dalton, M. (1959) *Men Who Manage*. Wiley, New York.

De Geer, H. *et al.* (1987) *In the Wake of the Future. Swedish Perspectives on the Problems of Structural Change*. Avebury, Aldershot; Brookfield, USA; Hong Kong; Singapore; Sydney.

Drucker, P.F. (1955) *The Practice of Management*. Heinemann, London.

Edström, A. (1985) *Leadership and Strategic Change*. Paper prepared for the International Human Resource Management Symposium at Fontainebleau, August 20–23, 1985. FArådet, Stockholm

Edström, A., Maccoby, M., Rendahl, J.E. and Strömberg, L. (1985) *Ledare för Sverige*. (In Swedish), ('Leaders for Sweden'.) Liber, Stockholm.

England, G.W. (1967) Personal value systems of American managers. *Academy of Management Journal*, **10** (1), 53–68.

Fayol, H. (1948) *Industrial and General Management*. Pitman, London.

Fiedler, F.E. (1967) *A Theory of Leadership Effectiveness*. McGraw-Hill, New York.

Forslin, J. (1989) *Frånngrottekvarn till lekstuga. En storindustri byter kultur* (in Swedish), (From Treadmill To Playhouse. A large Industrial Enterprise Changes its Culture). F Arådet, Stockholm.

Gellerman, S. (1968) *Management by Motivation.* American Management Association, New York.

Globerman, S. (1986) *Fundamentals of International Business Management.* Prentice Hall, Englewood Cliffs, New Jersey.

Granick, D. (1962) *The European Executive.* Weidenfeld & Nicholson, London.

Granick, D. (1972) *Management Comparisons in Four Developed Countries.* MIT Press, Cambridge, Massachusetts..

Graves, D. (1986) *Corporate Culture: Diagnosis and Change.* Francis Pinter, London.

Groves, A. (1983) *High Output Management.* Pan, London.

Hall, D.J., de Bettignies, H.C. and Amado-Fishgrund, G. (1969) 'The European Business Elite: an Exclusive Survey in Six European Countries 12, *European Business*, Vol. 23, pp. 52–61.

Hammond, V. (ed.)(1985) *Current Research in Management.* Association of Teachers of Management, Francis Pinter, London.

Handy, C., Gordon, C., Gow, G. and Randlesome, C. (1988) *Making Managers.* Pitman, London.

Hann, P. (1985) Umeo Oyama: This corporate doctor with homespun remedies is no quack. *International Management*, **53**.

Harbison, F.H. and Myers, C.A. (1959) *Management in the Industrial World.* McGraw-Hill, New York.

Hayes, C., Anderson, N. and Fonda, N. (1984) 'International Competition and the Role of Competence', *Personnel Management*. Sept., London.

Hersey, P. and Blanchard, K.H. (1982) *Management of Organizational Behavior,* 4th ed. Prentice-Hall, Englewood Cliffs, New Jersey.

Herzberg, F. (1968) *Work and the Nature of Man.* Staples Press, London.

Hickson, D.J. and McClelland, C.J. (eds) (1981) *Organization and Nation: the Aston Programme 4.* Gower, Aldershot.

Hofstede, G. (1980) *Culture's Consequences.* Sage, Beverly Hills, California.

Horne, J.H. and Lupton, T. (1965) 'The Work Activities of Middle Managers', *Journal of Management Studies,* Vol. 2 (No. 1), pp. 14–33.

Humble, J.W. (1973) *Improving the Performance of the Experienced Manager.* McGraw-Hill, New York.

Iacocca, L. (1984) *An Autobiography.* Bantam, New York.

Institute of Manpower Studies (1988) *Human Resourcing Strategies in Electronics: a Report for NEDO.* Sept., Falmer, Sussex.

Institute of Personnel Management (1988) *MBAs.* Personnel Management Fact Sheet No. 12, December. IPM, London.

Kanter, R.M. (1985) *The Change Masters: Corporate Entrepreneurs at Work.* George Allen and Unwin, London.

Kepner, C.H. and Tregoe, B.B. (1965) *The Rational Manager: A Systematic Approach to Problem-solving and Decision-making.* McGraw-Hill, New York.

Kharbanda, O.P. and Stallworthy, E.A. (1987) *Company Rescue: How to Manage a Business Turnaround.* Heinemann, London.

Kitromilides, P. (1981) Introductory essay: A perspective on the temper of twentieth-century European culture. In: Hoffman, S. and Kitromilides, P. (eds) *Culture and Society in Contemporary Europe: A Casebook.* George Allen and Unwin, London.

Koestler, A. (1975) *The Act of Creation*. Picador, London.

Kotler, P., Fahey, L. and Jatusripitak, S. (1985) *The New Competition: Meeting the Marketing Challenge from the Far East*. Prentice-Hall, Englewood Cliffs, New Jersey.

Laurent, A. (1985) The cultural diversity of Western conceptions of management. In: Joynt, P. and Warner, M. (eds) *Managing in Different Cultures*. Universitetsforlaget, Oslo.

Lawrence, P. (1986) *Management in the Netherlands: a Study in Nationalism*. Department of Management Studies, Loughborough University.

Lawrence, P.R. and Lorsch, J. (1967) *Organization and Environment*. Harvard Business School, Boston, Massachusetts.

Leavitt, H.J. (1986) *Corporate Pathfinders: Building Vision and Values into Organizations*. Dow-Jones-Irvin, Home Wood, Illinois.

Likert, R. (1961) *New Patterns of Management*. McGraw-Hill, London.

Lindkvist, L. (1988) *A Passionate Search for Nordisk Management*. Institute for Organization and Industrial Sociology, Copenhagen School of Economics. Samfundslitteratur, Copenhagen.

Lindsey, A.D. (1943) *The Modern Democratic State*. OUP. London

Lorenz, C. (1986) Management page. *Financial Times*, July 2nd, London.

Lundin, R.A. and Wirdenius, H. (1989) *Företagsförnyelse mot alla odds*. (In Swedish), ('Enterprise renewal against all odds.) FArådet and Swedish Building Research Council, Stockholm.

Lyons, T. (1976) *The Carroll Experiment*. ANCO, Dublin.

Lyons, T. (1981) The Kilkea design: A proven formula for an international development workshop. *Journal of European Training*, 5 (1).

McClelland, D.C. (1961) *The Achieving Society*. Van Nostrand, Princeton, New Jersey.

McKinseys (1988) *Performance and Competitive Success in the UK Electronics Industry: Part One – Strengthening the Competitiveness of UK Electronics*. NEDO. Falmer Sussex.

Maccoby, M. (1981) *The Leader: A New Face for American Management*. Simon & Schuster, New York.

McGregor, D. (1960) *The Human Side of Enterprise*. McGraw-Hill, New York.

Marples, D.L. (1967) Studies of managers: A fresh start? *Journal of Management Studies*, **10**, 282–99.

Maslow, A. (1970) *Motivation and Personality*. Harper & Row, New York.

Mintzberg, H. (1973) *The Nature of Managerial Work*. Harper & Row, New York.

Negandhi, A.R. and Prasad, S.B. (1971) *Comparative Management*. Appleton-Century-Crofts, New York.

Ouchi, W.G. (1981) *Theory Z: How American Business Can Meet the Japanese Challenge*. Addison-Wesley, Reading, Massachusetts.

Pahl, R.E. and Winkler, J.T. (1974) The economic élite: Theory and practice. In: Stanworth, P. and Giddens, A. (eds) *Elites and Power in British Society*.

Pascale, R.T. and Athos, A.G. (1980) *The Art of Japanese Management: Applications for American Executives*. Simon & Schuster, New York.

Peters, T.J. and Waterman, R.H. (1982) *In Search of Excellence: Lessons from America's Best-run Companies*. Harper & Row, New York.

Pollard, S. (1965) *The Genesis of Modern Management*. Edward Arnold, London.

Popper, K.R. (1960) *The Poverty of Historicism*, 2nd ed. Routledge and Kegan Paul, London.

Popper, K.R. (1963) *Conjectures and Refutations: The Growth of Scientific Knowledge*. Routledge and Kegan Paul, London.

Rall, W. (1986) Management page. *Financial Times*, July 2nd, London.

Rilke, R.M. (1934) *Letters to a Young Poet*. Norton, New York.

Rubenowitz, S. (1967) 'The Personnel Manager', paper presented at the Third International Conference of the European Association for Personnel Management (EAPM) in Stockholm 12-22 June.

Sayles, L.R. (1964) *Managerial Behavior: Administration in Complex Organizations*. McGraw-Hill, New York.

Sayles, L. (late 1960s) *Studies of Management in Business Schools*.

Schein, E.H. (1965) *Organizational Psychology*. Prentice-Hall, Englewood Cliffs, New Jersey.

Schein, E.H. (1985) *Organizational Culture and Leadership: A Dynamic View*. Jossey-Bass, San Francisco, California.

Schumpeter, J.A. (1942) *Capitalism, Socialism and Democracy*. Harper & Bros., New York.

Scott, J. F. and Lynton, R.P. (1952) *Three Studies in Management*. Routledge and Kegan Paul, London.

Simon, H.A. (1957) *Administrative Behavior*, 2nd ed. Macmillan, London.

Slatter, S. (1984) *Corporate Recovery: Successful Turnaround Strategies and their Implementation*. Penguin, London.

Sloan, A.P. (1963) *My years with General Motors*. Doubleday, Garden City, New York.

Spouster, J. (1984) *TQC Total Quality Control: An Australian Experience*. Horwitz Grahame, Melbourne.

Stam, J.A. (1982) *Human Resource Management in Japan: Organizational Innovation in Three Medium Sized Companies*. Erasmus University, Rotterdam.

Stewart, R. (1967) *Managers and their Jobs: A Study of the Similarities and Differences in the Ways Managers Spend Their Time*. Macmillan, London.

Takamiya, S. and Thurley, K.E. (eds) (1985) *Japan's Emerging Multi-nationals*. Tokyo University Press, Tokyo.

Thurley, K.E. (1988) 'Die kuftige Entwicklung der industriellen Demokratie und die Bedeutung der Erforschung der Function von Ingenieuren und mittlerem Management', in Fricke, W. and Jager, W. (eds) *Sozial-wissenschaften und Industrielle Demokratie*. Verlag Neue Gesellschaft, Gmbh, Bonn.

Thurley, K.E., Lam, A. and Lorriman, J. (1988) *The Development of Electronics Engineers: A Japanese/UK Comparison*. Suntory/Toyota International Centre for Economics and Related Disciplines. WP No. 179. London School of Economics.

Thurley, K.E. and Peccei, R. (1989) *Study on the Changing Functions of Lower and Middle Management*. Report on the work carried out and findings of Phase I, 1987/8. European Foundation, Dublin. (In press)

Thurley, K.E. and Wirdenius, H. (1973) *Supervision: A Reappraisal*. Heinemann, London.

Tichy, N. (1983) *Managing Strategic Change: Technical, Political and Cultural Dynamics*. Wiley, New York.

Trevor, M. (1988) *Toshiba's New British company: Competitiveness Through Innovation in Industry*. Policy Studies Institute, London.

Urwick, L.F. and Brech, E.F.L. (1947) *The Making of Scientific Management*. Management Publications, London.

Vroom, V.R. (1964) *Work and Motivation*. Wiley, New York.

Vroom, V.R. and Yetton, P.W. (1973) *Leadership and Decision-making*. University of Pittsburg.

Walker, C.R. (1968) *Technology, Industry and Man*. McGraw-Hill, New York.

Webb, S. (1917) *The Works Manager Today*. Longsman Green, London.

Webber, R.A. (1969) *Culture and Management: Text and Readings in Comparative Management*. Irwin, Homewood, Illinois.

Weber, Max (1967) *From Max Weber: Essays in Sociology*, translated and edited by Gerth, H.H. and Wright Mills, C., sixth edition. Routledge and Kegan Paul, London.

Weinshall, T.D. (ed.)(1977) *Culture and Management*. Penguin, London.

Whyte, W.F. (1955) *Money and Motivation*. Harper, New York.

Whyte, W.H. (1956) *Organization Man*. Simon and Schuster, New York.

Wiener, M. (1981) *English Culture and the Decline of the Industrial Spirit, 1850–1980*. Cambridge University Press.

Williamson, O.E. (1977) *Markets and Hierarchies: Analyses and Anti-trust Implications*. Free Press, New York.

Winkler, J.T. (1974) The ghost at the bargaining table: Directors and industrial relations. *British Journal of Industrial Relations*, **12**, July.

Woodward, J. (1965) *Industrial Organization: Theory and Practice*. Oxford University Press, Oxford.

Appendix

Analysis of production system management / supervisory management - a diagnostic scheme

A. 1 Describe economic and social background of company

Method

- Descriptive data

Criteria

- Industrial sector
- Trade position and outlook
- Formal company status, public/private, etc.
- Overall company performance: growth, profitability

A. 2 Select factory/establishment and describe characteristics

Method

- Descriptive data

Criteria

- Local community environment
- Relationship to overall enterprise

- Organizational chart
- Plans for future investment/change

A. 3 Break down each factory/establishment into a set of production systems

Method

- Outline work-flow chart

Criteria

- Interdependent production processes
- Recognized boundaries for control
- Recognized managerial authority system (areas of defined responsibilities)

(Production includes manufacture, transport, maintenance, service, etc.)

A. 4 Select production system

Method

- Detailed work-flow chart

Criteria

- Key set of operations needed for performance improvement

A. 5 Define degree of complexity of production system: describe and position system on five dimensions

Method

- Establish if it is a fragmented or integrated system (isolated operations, e.g. traditional craft, or extremely interdependent operations, e.g. aircraft flight operations).

Criteria

- Technical complexity (of process)
- Interdependence of operations (type and nature)
- External dependence (flow of components, power, environmental conditions, etc.)
- Proportion of non-programmed decisions (non-repetitive, one-off decisions)
- Relative changeability of product (batch size, product run times, etc.)

A. 6 Describe form of work organization

Method

- Descriptive, based on analysis of work undertaken - method study

Criteria

Nature of operative roles:
- Individual/group tasks
- Degree of repetitive work
- Skills required
- Degree of machine pacing
- Nature of production planning
- Criteria for selection of operatives

A. 7 Describe form of supervisory system

Method

- Management's perception/rating of supervision (their role and tasks; role requirements now and in the future)
- Payment
- Define levels/titles

- Define recruitment, selection, promotion policy

Criteria

- Number of status levels
- Specialist and generalist roles
- Job responsibilities
- Numbers supervised
- Relation with key staff departments

A. 8 Interview to define nature of steering function

Method

- Hard production performance data (output, quality, etc.)
- Personnel data
- Critical incident analysis (self-completion and interview)
- Attitude interview (attitudes to change, to company, to own job, what to improve)

Criteria

- Identify typical disturbances
- Supervisory actions
- Others' actions
- Solutions reached
- Preventive action taken, initiator of action
- Suggestions for improvement
- Perceived role now and in the future

A. 9 Prepare report

Method

- Written report using structure implied above

Criteria

- Describe and analyse information collected
- Describe problems that worry/concern supervisors, workers and managers
- Isolate problem areas where supervisory performance might be changed

Index

Abegglen, J., 32
American management, crucial ideas of, 19
American management, versus Japanese management, 19-20
Analysis-based strategy of change, 43
Ansoff, T.H., 35, 46
Argyris, C., 35
Assessment centres, 22
Athos, A.G., 2

Bakke, E.W., 34
Barnard, C., 26
Barnett, C., 6, 8
Basset, P., 21, 23
Beckard, R., 16, 35
Becker, G.S., 89
Beckérus, Å., 3
Bennis, W.G., 16, 35
Bettigniez, H.C.de, 32
Bingham, W.V., 34
Blake, R.R., 16, 31, 34
Blanchard, K.H., 19, 31, 32, 34
Brech, E.F.L., 31
Brooke, M., 4
Brown, W., 93, 100
'Bureaucratic phenomenon', 7-8
Burns, T., 8, 27, 34, 35, 89
Business unit, definition of, 28, 30

Carlson, S., 26, 34
Cartwright, D., 34
Chandler, A.D.Jr., 48
Change, motivation for, 43

Change, objectives for, 42-43, 79-80
Change strategies, 43
Change strategy, design of, 51-52
'Company doctor' solution, 9-10
Crozier, M., 7, 8, 10
Cuckney, J., 9
Cyert, R.M., 35

Dahrendorf, R., 14
Dalton, M., 34
De Geer, H., 3
Deming, W., 75
Diös case, 52-62
Drucker, P.F., 16, 31, 35

Edström, A., 3, 34
Empirical-rational strategy of change, 44-45
England, G.W., 32, 35
Enterprise management, definition of, 29-30
Enterprise management, forms of, 48-49
Enterprise management, functions of, 49-50
Enterprise management, strategy of, 52
European Community, 4-7, 90-91
European management, definition of, 2-4
European management, model of strategic change, 100-101
European management, suggested model, 97-101
European manager, career path for, 101-102
Evaluation of change programme, 45-46

Fahey, L., 10
Fayol, H., 2, 26, 31, 35
Fiedler, F.E., 34
Forslin, J., 67

Gellerman, S., 16, 31
Gilbreth, F.B., 26
Globerman, D., 3
Granick, D., 2, 32
Graves, D., 32, 39
Guru phenomenon, 18

H form organization, 48
Hann, P., 9
Harbison, F.H., 32, 38, 90
Hawthorne-effect, in evaluation of change, 46

Head hunting, 23
Herzberg, F., 32, 34
Hickson, D.J., 32
Hofstede, G., 32, 35
Horne, J.H., 27
Human relations leadership, 66-67
Humble, J.W., 31

Iacocca, L., 17, 34
ICI case, 68-75
Input efficiency, 66
INSEAD, 12
Internationalization strategies, 95-96

Japanese management, crucial ideas of, 20
Japanese management, versus American management, 19-20
Jatusripitak, S., 10
Johnson, S., 19, 31, 32
Just-in-time system, 22

Kepner, C.H., 31, 35
Kharbanda, O.P., 9
Kilkea case, 77-78
Kitromilides, P., 6
'Knowledge in use', of managers, 41, 47
Kotler, P., 10

Lam, A., 8
Laurent, A., 12, 13
Lawrence, P.R., 33, 35
Leavitt, H.J., 16
Likert, R., 31, 32, 34
Lindkvist, L., 3
Lindsey, A.D., 83
Lorenz, 17, 18
Lorriman, J., 8
Lorsch, J., 33, 35
Lundin, R.A., 52
Lupton, T., 27, 34
Lyons, T., 76, 77

M form organization, 48
Maccoby, M., 3, 34
Macgregor, I., 9
Management, definition of, 27-30

Management theory, as perceived by practicing managers, 37
Management theory, classification of, 33-36
Management, viability of, 90-93
Manager, definition of, 25-26
Manager reward systems, 21-22
Managerial élite, 14
Managerial identities, 13
Managerial legitimacy, creation of, 99-101
Managerial role, conceptions of, 12-13
Managerial role, studies of, 26-27
March, J.G., 35
Marples, D.L., 34
Maslow, A., 32
McClelland, C.J., 32
McClelland, D.C., 32
McGregor, D., 32, 34
Meta-evaluation of change, 46
Method-based strategy of change, 43-45
Mintzberg, H., 27, 34, 35
Mouton, J.S., 16, 31
Myers, C.A., 32, 38, 90
Möstl, E., 18

Neghandi, A.R., 33

Operational management, definition of, 29-30
Operational management, functions of, 50
Organization development, 67, 68-75
Ouchi, W.G., 2, 31
Output efficiency, 66
Oyama, U., 9

Pascale, R.T., 2
Peccei, R., 5
Peters, T.J., 2, 17, 31, 89
Pollard, S., 25
Popper, K.R., 31, 98
Power-based strategy of change, 43-45
Problem solution strategy of change, 43-45
Production system, definition of, 28
Production system, types of, 79
Production systems, social context of, 63-65

Quality circles, 22, 33, 38, 75-76
Quality of work life (QWL) indicators, 67

Quality of work life (QWL) objectives, 80
Quality standards movements, 22

Rall, W., 17
Rendahl, J.E., 3
Rilke, R.M., 6
Rowen, 26
Rubenowitz, S., 33

Sayles, L.R., 27, 34
Schein, E.H., 16, 35
Schumpeter, J.A., 35
Service management courses, 22
Simon, H.A., 35, 39
Slatter, S., 9
Sloan, A.P., 31, 33, 34
Socio-technical redesign, 67
Spouster, J., 75
Stallworthy, E.A., 9
Stalker, G.M., 8, 35, 89
Stam, J.A., 33
Stewart, R., 27, 34
Strategies of change, 43
Strategy of change, design of, 51-52, 80-82
Strategy of change, model of, 100-101
Strömberg, L., 3
Supervisory management, definition of, 28-30
Supervisory management, diagnostic scheme, 113-117
Supervisory management, functions of, 50, 65-66
Supervisory management, improvement of, 66-76
Supervisory management, regeneration of, 79-85
System efficiency, 66

Takamiya, S., 21
Taylor, F.W., 26
Theory X and Y, 32
Third-party role, at change, 46-47
Thulliez, G., 17
Thurley, K.E., 5, 8, 21, 34, 76, 93
Tichy, N., 35
Total Quality Control (TQC), 22, 33, 75-76, 83
Total Quality Control (TQC), objectives of, 80
Tregoe, B.B., 31, 35
Trevor, M., 23

Urwick, L.F., 2, 31, 33

Vroom, V.R., 32, 34

Walker, C.R., 34
Waterman, R.H., 2, 17, 31, 89
Webb, S., 25
Webber, R.A., 32
Weber, M., 2
Weinshall, T.D., 32
Whyte, W.H., 34
Wiener, M., 63
Williamson, O.E., 48
Wirdenius, H., 34, 52, 76
Woodward, J., 33, 35, 77

Yetton, P.W., 34
Young, A., 16

Zero defects, 22, 33, 76